He Took My Kidney,
Then Broke My Heart

Also available:

'Dave Spikey – Best Medicine Tour Live' DVD

He Took My Kidney, Then Broke My Heart

Dave Spikey

Michael O'Mara Books Limited

First published in Great Britain in 2009 by
Michael O'Mara Books Limited
9 Lion Yard
Tremadoc Road
London SW4 7NQ

ISBN: 978-1-84317-385-4

1 3 5 7 9 10 8 6 4 2

Designed by Burville-Riley Partnership

Printed and bound in Great Britain by Clays Ltd, St Ives plc

www.mombooks.com

FOREWORD

I've always loved local newspapers. I love how they prioritize the news from the local area above national and global events. Those stories are always relegated to a couple of columns inside – and I love how, even in those sparse acknowledgements of the wider world, the papers often manage to crowbar in a local reference: 'Earthquake in Peru – Hundreds Feared Dead – No Bolton People Involved.'

I love the local 'Poets' Corner', where the poems are so bad they are good. I love the classified ads, where I once saw:

> **FORD FIESTA**, 1995, low mileage, 1 lady owner, taxed and MOT 12 months, £3,995.
> **FORD MONDEO**, red, 1997, 72,000 miles, FSH £5,400 ono.
> **FORD ALBERT**, peacefully in hospital. Albert dearly loved husband, father and brother, etc.

They'd put an obituary in 'Cars for Sale'!

Talking of obituaries, though, have you ever seen those cringeworthy rhyming obituaries? Why do people do that?

> Tears and flowers are all we can share
> For today's your birthday
> And you're not there.

Well, obviously! How insensitive can you get just for a rhyme? You can almost see Aunty Marj – who has been given the job of family poet laureate because she once had a poem in 'Poets' Corner' about Lady Di (in which she'd probably rhymed 'Di' with 'die') – sat at home chewing the end of her pencil, desperate for some inspiration. 'Now what rhymes with "tumour"? Got it! Old Tommy had a sense of humour, get in!'

My favourite headline from *The Bolton News* was 'Dead Man Weds' (which, as some of you may know, provided the inspiration for my local-newspaper-based ITV1 sitcom of the same name). What was great about this front-page headline, of course, was the absence of any inverted commas around the word 'dead', so it read like a dead man had actually got married – as opposed to the real story, which concerned a man who had suffered a cardiac arrest some months earlier, who had been brought back from death by the paramedics and was now sufficiently recovered to get married.

When I saw it, once I'd got over my initial shock and amusement, I did have a moment when I thought, 'No, hang on, this *is* Bolton, he could actually be dead.' I pictured the scene at the wedding reception ...

> **Man:**
> *The groom's not saying much.*
>
> **Woman:**
> *He's dead.*
>
> **Man:**
> *Is he?*
>
> **Woman:**
> *Yeah, but they'd ordered the buffet from Mollie Bentham's, so ...*
>
> **Man:**
> *They'd lose the deposit.*
>
> **Woman:**
> *Yeah. Pass us a mini quiche.*

On my latest 'Best Medicine' stand-up tour, I decided to incorporate my love of local newspapers into my routine. I planned to obtain copies of the local rags from each town or city in which I appeared, hoping that

I might find a regional story or two that I could highlight on stage and milk for comedy value. I anticipated that this would be a hit-and-miss affair; that I might find only the odd story or article, maybe one every other gig.

How wrong I was! I found loads and *loads* of stories. To the locals, they might have seemed run-of-the-mill, but to an outsider, as I was, seeing events through different eyes proved ... well, if not hilarious, then at the very least highly amusing.

I collected all the articles along the way – from local papers, national rags and online news services – and I've put them in this book. There are bizarre stories ('"Fun" with Ferrets at the YMCA'), stranger-than-fiction true tales ('Man Dressed as Grim Reaper Arrested'), badly worded captions and headlines, and unbelievable page fillers (from those weeks when a paper must *really* have been struggling for content). I feature them all here ... along with my comedy take on them. I hope you enjoy them.

Personally, I think that they not only illustrate community life throughout the United Kingdom wonderfully, but also – as I've discovered when performing some of them live on stage – they underline one of the greatest attributes of our nation: we aren't afraid to laugh at ourselves.

Dave Spikey, 2009

COPS NAB FIVE TEEN DRUNKS A DAY

Sunderland Echo

It's *fifteen* – five teen isn't a number, even in the North-East.

PUB STAYS OPEN

Herts Advertiser

Another temporary tenant has been parachuted into a country pub while the sale of the premises is negotiated.

The previous tenants of the popular pub in School Lane, Gary and Sandra Higinbotham, were evicted last summer ...

... after falling behind with rent payments, which they said were impossible to meet with the amount of trade they turned over. ■

Who'd be mad enough to buy a place where you have to parachute in?

Fired them out of a cannon, I expect.

If people have to skydive into a pub, you're not going to get much passing trade, are you?

Milkman puts out shop fire with 320 pints

Daily Telegraph

A milkman on his early morning round put out a fire in a shop by dousing it with milk.

How long did that take? Go to milk float, take bottle out of crate, take top off, run to fire, pour on fire. Hang on, I'm going to try it.

.

..

...

Sorry about that, I dropped one ... but it averages out at about five seconds per bottle – call it six because you've got to build in a factor for removing empty crates (and it makes the calculation easier), so in total it took him 32 minutes – over half an hour. I would have thought the fire would have taken hold by then (and still no sign of the fire brigade).

With the help of two postmen ...

See, I wish I'd read that bit before I tried my experiment. There were three of them!

I'd like to know exactly how they tackled the blaze. Did they form a human chain passing the bottles down the line, or did they individually run like maniacs back and forth to the milk float? I'd also like to know what two postmen were doing on the same street ...

Steven Leach, 35, poured 320 pints onto the flames at Magpies gift shop in Redruth, Cornwall. He was named Hero Milkman of the Millennium by the National Dairymen's Association.

Whoa! 'Hero Milkman of the Millennium'? That's 'the *Millennium*'. Hell of a title. It does beg the question, though: hasn't a milkman done anything else at all heroic in the last thousand years?

Mr Leach said yesterday, 'The smoke was very thick and some of the milk was burning, but we carried on until the fire brigade arrived.'

'Hero Milkman of the Millennium' or not, he missed a trick. He should have chucked all his eggs and butter on as well, so that when the firefighters arrived, they could all have had a lovely custard.

John Ward, boss of the Unigate / Dairy Crest depot in nearby Camborne ...

You know, 'Gullible' John Ward?

... said, 'Afterwards, he carried on with his round.

He had milk left?!

'We only heard about it when he filled in a report to say where the 320 pints had gone.'

It all sounds a bit fishy now ...

Scene: Unigate / Dairy Crest Depot HQ

Gullible John Ward:
I've been reading your report, Leach, and it appears that you are 320 pints short?

Steven Leach:
If you turn over, you'll see ...
(John Ward turns over)

Steven Leach:
No, not you, the report. Turn that over.
(Thinks: 'How did he ever get to be a manager?')

Gullible John Ward:
(Turns report over and reads)
You poured it on a fire?

Steven Leach:
Yes, I did.

Gullible John Ward:
Well done. I wouldn't be surprised if this put you in the running for 'Hero Milkman of the Millennium'.

Steven Leach:
Just doing my duty, sir. Anyone would have done the same.

Meanwhile, the newly blonde divorcee at number 38 is bathing in semi-skimmed ...

JACKSIE POTATO

The Sun

A vicar turned up in agony at a hospital – with a potato stuck in his bottom.

Hence headline 'JACKSIE POTATO'. A headline writer's dream, it has to be said. If I may, I submit for your consideration 'SPUD YOU LIKE' and – arguably better – 'POTATO WEDGIE' ... I thank you.

The clergyman told stunned casualty nurses he fell backwards onto his kitchen table while hanging curtains. He happened to be nude at the time.

The old 'hanging curtains in the nude' excuse. What a shot, though! The spud could have gone anywhere, but no ... 'One hundred and eighty! Vicar, you require double top – ooh, unlucky: single bottom.' Straight in. Be even more impressive if it was a King Edward.

The red-faced vicar ...

Not just his face, I'll wager.

14

... insisted to staff at the (Sheffield) Northern General Hospital that his predicament was NOT the result of a sex game gone wrong.

Which spud-based sex game would that be? 'One potato, two potato, three potato – four. One potato up my bottom, one potato more'?

A&E nurse Trudi Watson said, 'He explained to me quite sincerely he had been hanging curtains naked in the kitchen ...

Please! Think of the neighbours. 'Maureen? The vicar's at the kitchen window with his meat and two veg out again – no, hang on! Three veg.'

'... when he fell backwards onto the kitchen table and onto a potato.'

You say, 'Potato'; I say, 'Po-dildo ...'

She admitted some sex-related emergencies had made staff chuckle, but she urged anyone sticking something where the sun don't shine to think again. Ms Watson said, 'My advice? Don't do it.'

That's incisive. Let me just get a pen to write that professional medical advice down.

The embarrassed reverend in his fifties had to undergo a delicate operation to extract the offending vegetable.

Whoa! Red card, ref! Less of the 'offending' and more of the 'innocent bystander' vegetable, please: lying about in the vegetable rack minding its own business one minute, the next ... it's spud's eye to Jap's eye.

As for the delicate operation, I'd like to think they used a microwave.

The spud was yesterday revealed to be among a litany of objects that medics in Sheffield have removed from people's nether regions. Others include a can of deodorant ...

'A can of deodorant'? Ouch. I'd accept one of those underarm rollette things. Well, when I say 'accept' ...

... a cucumber and a Russian doll.

A hospital trust spokesperson in Sheffield said, 'Like all busy hospitals, we do see some unusual accidents. But our staff deal with them in a discreet, professional and kind way.'

◼

A Russian doll! That's a brilliant idea on paper, isn't it? Ticks the boxes – required shape and size (I imagine) – but the bloke's not really thought it through, has he? I take you now to Sheffield Northern General Hospital.

Scene: Operating Theatre

Doctor:
Okay, I'm in. I've got the forceps round the object – it looks like a doll! So if I gently twist and pull and ... Yes, it's coming ... There it is! Gotcha! Oh, hang on – there's another one up there: bit more tricky, this, because it's slightly smaller. Gently does it. Yes, I've got it! Oh, what? There's another!

Discreet? It's in the bloody *Sun*!

Dogged determination of savaged MP earns him praise from the boss

Stockport Express

Reddish MP Andrew Gwynne suffered a savaging on the doorstep when he was bitten by a dog.

The MP discovered just how vicious politics can get when he pushed an election leaflet through a letter box in Audenshaw. The dog, which was on the other side of the door, sank its teeth into the MP's left index finger and refused to let go.

That's twice they've said 'savaged' — must have been terrible.

His left index finger – *savaged*. So this needs immediate action, obviously, and surely there's no one better qualified to provide a quick, incisive (sorry) and intelligent response than a Member of Parliament. I bet you can't guess what he did next. This is funny ...

Mr Gwynne, 33, put his right hand through the letter box to goad the dog into releasing his left hand . . .

Good move: goad the dog. What was going through his tiny mind? Strange, though, it didn't work. Go on, guess what happened next. This is even funnier. This is double funny.

. . . only for the angry animal to bite at that one instead.

No! Who'd have thought? (Pause for big F. Off Laugh.)

Mr Gwynne said, 'The dog didn't even bark . . .

Sneaky buggers, dogs.

'. . . it just pounced from nowhere.

What does he mean 'it just pounced from nowhere'? Define 'nowhere', Mr Gwynne – it was on the other side of the door, in its house, where it lives.

'Luckily, adrenalin kicked in and I managed to prise its jaws open. I managed to stem the bleeding with a tissue.

It took a full tissue to stem the bleeding. That's proper savaged.

'My finger had been well chewed as if I'd dunked it in a blender.'

Oh come on, behave! A tissue stemmed the bleeding. You'd need a bath towel if you stuck your hand in a blender.

Mind you, he is an MP, remember. So he's probably being economical with the truth and ... he probably *has* dunked his hand in a blender.

11-YEAR-OLD'S HAND SAVAGED BY DOG

Oldham Evening Chronicle

A Japanese Akita dog, which attacked a schoolboy and left him with 19 stitches in his right hand, has been destroyed.

Benjamin Barratt-Maher (11) was walking with his great-grandfather Frank Barratt (77) and brother Lewis (4) when the dog attacked.

Benjamin said he was nipping across open land to look at cars in a Scouthead garage when the sleeping dog woke up and fastened its jaws around his hand.

'Savaged' again.

Nineteen stitches – that's more like it. You listening, Mr Gwynne? No mention of stitches in your 'savaging'.

Well, they say 'attacked'. You read on and make your own mind up.

Mr Barratt said, 'One moment I was talking to Lewis about the sheep and the animals and the next thing I know, Benjamin is screaming and it looked like the dog was hanging from his arm.'

Benjamin hit the dog with a bone he had found.

Benjamin added, 'There was a brick near by, but I thought that would hurt him too much.'

'It *looked like* the dog was hanging from his arm.' What else did you think it could be? A big furry scarf?

A bone! Oh, it's getting clearer now. Let's have a quick recap: the dog's asleep, it wakes up and sees an eleven-year-old kid stood there, holding its ... bone ... Grrrrrrr.

The kid's an idiot. There's this huge (and they are huge) Japanese Akita, which according to his great-granddad is 'hanging from his arm', and he's torn (in more ways than one), thinking, 'Brick? Bone? Bone? Brick? Oh, I don't know ... Er, bone!' He's got a future in politics, this lad.

His mother called for stronger action against dangerous dog owners. She said, 'The police told me that because the dog was chained and on private land, it was not covered by the Dangerous Dogs Act.'

■

So that's 'chained' and 'on private land'. To summarize, then, they were trespassing and for some mad reason approached a huge sleeping dog, which was well chained up. They went closer than was sensible and woke the dog up, possibly by picking up its bone. It wasn't happy and now it's less happy because it's dead. They got away lightly, I reckon.

So ... Dangerous Dogs

I highlight these two stories from the tour because – without exaggeration – the local newspapers carried a dangerous dog story in one in three gigs.

I also read during that time that there was legislation in the pipeline to castrate dangerous dogs. I immediately thought, 'No – take their teeth out! It's the teeth that do the damage.' You never get a pit bull-type dog hurtling at you, barking like a banshee and then banging its bollocks up against you. 'Ouch' – now you're hopping around on one leg, holding your shin with one hand – 'That hurt! That's a dangerous dog, that!'

They had the president of some bull terrier association on television the other month. He was sat there on the sofa with this big, muscle-bound, pit bull-type dog. I can't remember what it was called – something beginning with 'A' – Attila or Adolf (pretty sure it wasn't Alan).

Anyway, you know that they say that owners look like their dogs? Well, he did: he was a big, ugly brute of a man with a dotted-line tattoo round his neck, and what looked like 'JIZ' tattooed on his arm (but turned out to be 'JIM' that had got a bit infected), and he had 'LOVE' and 'HATE' on his knuckles. Well, I say 'HATE', but he had a finger missing – maybe Alan had bitten it off at some stage – so he just had 'HAT' on that hand. 'LOVE' and 'HAT'? Not very scary, is it?

So anyway, he says there's undeserved hysteria regarding these 'lovable' dogs. He doesn't understand why people panic when a pit bull attacks. (Me neither: wimps.) He says that if a pit bull attaches itself to your leg – which they are prone to do – all you have to do is pour water down its nose and it thinks it's drowning, so it can't breathe and opens its mouth and drops off. 'Ha, ha, Mr Pit Bull!'

But what are the chances that you'll have some water on you? Zero. Going for a walk in the park? 'Got my gloves, got my book, got my reading glasses ... Is that it? Oh no! Water! Nearly forgot the water.'

The chances are that a pit bull will pounce when you are unprepared. It is a well-known fact that pit bulls will only attack you when they feel like it, and there it is, clamped on your leg with you feeling a proper fool for forgetting the jug of water.

I was thinking that if you were a bloke, you could pee down its nose. But that would take some bottle, wouldn't it? Getting your knob out in that situation. And it's likely that because of the shock, you wouldn't be able to wee, so you'd whistle to help it happen, but the whistling would attract another pit bull ... Oh no!

I have my own theory that I hope you never have to try, but I read somewhere that dogs hate poo being thrown at them. So, if a vicious pit bull ever attacks you, barking, slavering and baring its teeth, I'd suggest you throw a handful of poo at it.

I know you're thinking, 'What if there isn't any poo?'

To which I reply, 'Don't worry, there will be.'

Man dressed as Grim Reaper arrested

Morecambe Visitor

A man standing outside Morecambe police station dressed as the 'Grim Reaper' was arrested after a drunken night that went from bad to worse.

What comes after 'worse'? I ask because I think it went from bad to worse and then on to whatever comes after worse.

Christopher Kelly, 31, had come to Morecambe on October 5 with a group of friends from Nelson and got extremely drunk on lager and vodka.

So, he and his mates from Nelson, Lancashire chose Morecambe for a lads' night out. Not Prague, not Lisbon, not Dublin – Morecambe. So, we've established he's an idiot.

Kelly lost his mates, who were celebrating a friend's birthday and were also drunk . . .

He gets drunk, fair play, but then he loses his mates. You can't lose anybody in Morecambe! It's empty, deserted; you just go out onto the promenade and shout.

... and wandered onto the beach, where he got stuck in boggy sand and lost his shoes, trousers and jacket.

So he goes on the beach and sinks in the quicksand. Brilliant.

He takes his trousers off in order to escape. I don't know what might have prompted this, what his train of thought might have been. Maybe he was thinking back to his school swimming lessons and, getting that sinking feeling, removed his trousers to inflate as a float.

Cold and wet, he staggered across the road to Morecambe Town Hall ...

The Town Hall? Oh yes, of course, it's obvious! It's like if you're in trouble abroad, you head for the British Embassy. But what happens next is a disgrace and makes you despair at the state of our society.

... where, seeing a window open, he climbed inside.

Someone's left a bloody window open! In the Town Hall!

There, he went in various rooms, took a camera and a mobile phone, which he tried to use to call his friends.

So our pant-less, shoe-less hero climbs in (naturally) and searches for a mobile phone so that he can call his mates. First he finds a camera, but he can't get a signal on that and so he hunts some more and finds a mobile phone.

Now, I've never been in Morecambe Town Hall, but I'm guessing more or less every office in there has got an ordinary phone! But this dumbo looks for a mobile to call his mates.

You can take the bloke out of Nelson ...

Then he soiled his underwear ...

... which he threw into a black bin bag.

Fair play, he puts the offending underwear in a bin bag (tidy) and searches for something to wear.

He found a 'Grim Reaper' fancy-dress outfit and put this on ...

He finds a 'Grim Reaper' outfit? Course he does! There's a Grim Reaper costume in the Town Hall ... Good folk of Morecambe, what sort of people are running your town?

It's not clear from the report as to whether he had a choice of costumes: if, for instance, he rejected a clown or a cowboy outfit in the process. In retrospect, I think he should have gone for the policeman's uniform – that would have been funny, particularly given his next move ...

… before leaving the Town Hall and wandering down Lord Street towards Poulton Square, where he eventually arrived at the police station which was, at that time, unmanned. He stood there for three hours, still in the Grim Reaper gear, until police arrived.

Oh yes, he climbs back out of the window and wanders, dressed as the Grim Reaper, to the police station, but ... it's shut! Morecambe police station shuts at night when the town – full of drunks from Nelson – needs it most.

So he stands outside for three hours waiting for it to open – still in his Grim Reaper costume, remember. I was thinking that during that time he might have tried to hitch a lift, but you wouldn't stop for him, would you? I won't stop for those dodgy-looking blokes holding licence plates, never mind pulling over to give Death a lift home.

As the tale was being outlined by prosecutor Peter Bardsley at Lancaster Magistrates' Court on Friday, one probation service officer had to leave the courtroom in a fit of laughter.

Mr Bardsley said some of Kelly's antics in the Town Hall were captured on CCTV . . .

. . . and added: 'He didn't remember why he stole the camera and the phone, but remembers taking an item of clothing but not where he found it. He was cold and very drunk.'

Defending, John Lee said: 'This is a strange case, one which has caused hilarity, but is serious. In interview he made a full and frank admission that he was drunk and entered the Town Hall as a trespasser. The camera and mobile phone were recovered, but the Grim Reaper outfit was disposed of.'

Every credit. I laughed so much when I first read it that stuff came down my nose.

'Antics'?

I think we know why, don't we? Two words: soiled underpants. Now add to this two words notable by their absence: toilet paper.

Customer hit on head during fracas

Skegness Target

I think this is my favourite newspaper name ... and 'fracas': that's a word we need to see more of in the headlines these days.

Ivan Holmes-Parker (27) was already banned from 'The Vine' when he called in at the pub just after midnight.

A hyphenated name doesn't guarantee class.

Holmes-Parker and his partner Lisa Smith (26), of the same address, became aggressive and started shouting when they were refused service. A salt pot and a glass were thrown during the disturbance.

It's like the Bronx in Skegness! A salt pot and a glass! Not for them the grabbing of a whisky bottle and smashing it on the edge of the table, or breaking a chair over an assailant's back. No, I'm going to chuck this, er ... let's see ... salt pot.

Both were ordered to take part in the enhanced thinking skills programme.

Enhanced thinking skills lesson, part one: a cruet set is not an effective weapon.

WALKERS CRISPS WIPE ANGLESEY OFF THE MAP

North Wales Daily Post

Walkers Crisps have taken a bite out of the map of Great Britain, removing Anglesey from the British Isles in a tourism promotion. Walkers Crisps last night apologized to the people of Anglesey, but said the map was 'diagrammatic' and not 'geographic'.

I.T. worker Gareth Jones, who lives outside Bodedern ...

... said, 'I like Walkers Crisps, they make very nice crisps, but I will think twice about buying them next time I am in a shop ...

This would be down to the limited release of their new 'Enriched Uranium' flavour?

And that explanation, Mr Walker, is 'bollocks' not 'genitalia'.

Where exactly? Bodedern's a big place ... for Anglesey. Or does he actually live outside? I.T. work doesn't pay much in Wales.

(Outside Bodedern.)

'If they want to forget about us then we could forget about them for a while, at least until they change this map.

Sounds like a plan, Gareth.

'We don't want to become the forgotten people of Great Britain.

Steady on, son, it's only crisps.

'After all, there are 70,000 people living here and we are one of the main tourist places in Wales.'

But be fair, you have to have the weather.

Gareth has already lodged two complaints with Walkers Crisps, but Anglesey still remains absent from the British Isles map.
■

I don't know what to suggest, Gareth. If they've not acted after two complaints, they're not going to act now.

I'm personally not surprised – after all, you're dealing here with a company that unilaterally dismantled the traditional crisp packet colouring system without any public consultation. Since time began, a blue packet of crisps has indicated 'Salt and Vinegar' and a green packet was ... (interactive quiz element here) ... 'Cheese and Onion' (correct). And what did the despots at Walkers do? Switch them over.

So I know losing Anglesey off the map is hard to swallow – but more so is a salt-and-vinegar crisp when you were expecting cheese and onion.

NB: I think crisp manufacturers have missed a monumental trick ... and I hereby copyright my idea and invention of the packet of assorted crisps: the selection box of crisps. A bag full of every different flavour of crisp; like a lovely box of Milk Tray, but with the added excitement of not knowing which flavour you might savour next (because you can't identify a crisp like you can a chocolate). So every crisp is a delicious surprise – with the salt-and-vinegar crisp assuming the role of the coffee cream. It's an absolute winner and will make my fortune.

Tripping claims payouts down to £2m a year

Salford Advertiser

Only £2 million?! Excuse my French, but clumsy bastards. Whatever happened to accidents? If I trip up in the street, my main worry is 'Has anybody seen me?'

I'm sick to death of the 'Blame and Claim' ads. 'I was walking across reception when I slipped on some liquid ...' Look where you're going, you dozy cow! Liquid? It's a pool the size of Lake Windermere!

Or what about him? 'I was using a ladder without the appropriate instructions.' It's a ladder. What instructions? Did it not have 'STOP' at the top of it? Do you think the idiot had it lying horizontally for ages, muttering to himself, 'I don't get these ladders, they're not very high, are they? I should have had appropriate instructions.' How can he not know how to use a ladder?

My favourite – jaw-droppingly stupid – blame-and-claim case of recent years was when an old couple bought a motor home, a Winnebago, in which they planned to tour extensively. On delivery, they took it out for a test drive. The husband, who was driving, got it up to 70 mph on the motorway and then ... and then ... he put it in cruise control and nipped in the back to make a brew!

All I can think is that he thought cruise control was autopilot, but I have a brilliant picture of him in my head, pressing the cruise-control button, standing and stretching briefly, before moving off into the back with a 'What do you fancy, Doreen? Tea or coffee?'

CRAAAAASH!!

So he sued Winnebago and won substantial damages – because there is nothing in the instruction book that says that you cannot do this!

GNOME ATTACK

The Sun

A grandmother knocked out a burglar by hitting him with a garden gnome.

Jean Collop, 69, woke at 5 a.m. to find an intruder clambering on her roof.

She yelled at the man, then picked up a garden gnome and hurled it at him. It bounced off his head, leaving him lying dazed on the roof in Wadebridge, Cornwall.

He'll probably sue her. That's how it works – whiplash, stress, depression, 'she's ruined his life'.

So not technically an 'intruder'. Just a bloke on her roof. He's gonna take her to the cleaners ...

What a shot! I'm not a gnome aficionado, but I expect they are reasonably heavy – and this sixty-nine-year-old granny hit a bloke on her roof square on the head with one! She could try that another hundred times and I bet she wouldn't come close.

Jean dashed to fetch her rolling pin and a camera, and then took pictures of the burglar as neighbours called the police.

Again, Jean, not technically a 'burglar' – still just a bloke on your roof.

Jean said, 'I heard a crash and rushed out in my nightdress. I politely told him not to move and grabbed the first thing that came to hand, which was a garden gnome.

You can actually see what's happened during her statement, can't you? She's suddenly realized he could be on to Claims Direct first thing, so now it's 'I politely told him not to move and grabbed the first thing that came to hand' – a dramatic change from the original: 'She yelled at the man, then picked up a garden gnome and hurled it at him.'

'When it hit him, he lay down for a while. I got my rolling pin just in case. I didn't want to break another gnome.'
■

She dashes into the kitchen looking for another weapon … ignores the knives and heavy pans and goes straight for the rolling pin. Makes you proud to be British. In Chicago, the old dear would have blown him away with a Magnum, but over here the weapons of choice are gnomes and rolling pins. Just wonderful!

Gnomes banned from graveyard

Weston & Somerset Mercury

Diocesan chiefs have outlawed the positioning of the diminutive figurines to 'preserve the dignity' of churchyards. A spokesman for the Diocese of Bath and Wells said, 'Garden gnomes are certainly banned. They are non-creative beings and are not real.

'They are not part of the normal world ...

' ... they just don't exist.'

■

When you say 'non-creative', Mr Spokesman, do you mean in an artistic sense or as part of creation? If it's the latter, then yeah, 'non-creative' and 'not real' sort of go hand in hand.

Whereas angels and gargoyles ...? You allow them; can't move for 'em.

What arrogance! On what evidence do you base such an inflammatory statement? I put it to you that I personally have sincere faith that gnomes do exist and so, by utilizing your very own patented 'God' model, that is all I and like-minded people need.

We firmly believe that they are part of the goblin family, which also includes elves, pixies, fairies and leprechauns, not to mention trolls (I told you not to mention trolls).

We believe that they are all, for the most part (with the exception of the mistakenly aforementioned trolls, who live under bridges and can be quite unpleasant), friendly woodland dwellers who bring happiness and peace to the world and so – by using your criteria – that's all we need.

We also offer more compelling scientific evidence, which relates to the blueprint for all human life, which is known as the Human Genome. That's G-nome – and it's not a coincidence.

WOMAN WHO STOLE GNOMES FACES JAIL

Daily Telegraph

Karen Stenhouse, 37, crept into gardens within a 20-mile radius of her home and then sold the gnomes at car boot sales and street markets. The mother of three was caught by an 11-day undercover operation that led police to a horde of garden ornaments, including 30 gnomes.

They had an eleven-day undercover operation for this?! How 'undercover', exactly? I reckon it must have been a specially selected squad. You know that bit at the beginning of *Hill Street Blues*, where all the cops are given their missions? Must have gone a bit like this …

Scene: Police HQ

Sergeant:
'Titch' McKay? Bring your fishing rod. 'Shorty' Murdoch? Find the biggest mushroom you can. The rest of you: put on these blue tunics and red floppy hats. And hey! Let's be careful down there.

Stenhouse admitted six charges of stealing gnomes, plant pots, pots of flowers and garden ornaments from addresses in Alva, Tullibody, Stirling and Bridge of Allan.

Sheriff William Gilchrist deferred sentence for a background report.

One of Stenhouse's victims said, 'I lost a little old man smoking a pipe and an old lady with a barrow.'

◼

Or Gnome Country, as it's also known. Wild and untamed.

See? So wild and untamed that they have a sheriff: Wild Bill Gilchrist.

It's worse than we thought: she's taking little old people now! Police are asking everyone to be vigilant and are stressing that if anyone offers you a pipe-smoking old man at a car boot sale, you should call 999 immediately.

When NOT to call 999

www.thisislocallondon.co.uk

Only 17 per cent of 999 calls received in the last year were deemed worthy of an emergency response.

Examples of inappropriate 999 calls to Bromley police in the last year:

- Individuals called asking to get a taxi.

  Actually, this is easily done, especially if there is a local *6Nines* taxi firm.

- A woman called the emergency line to ask if officers could pop round to her house to pick up her dogs and drop them off at a relative's, because she was staying in hospital overnight.

  Give her a break. She's going into hospital, she's nervous, worried, confused – she meant to call Canine-nine-nine, the dog emergency hot line.

41

- A man called to say that the trains on the line behind his house were making a 'clink clunk clink clunk' noise instead of the usual 'click click click click'.

He's right, they definitely shouldn't be 'clunking' – but I'm not sure they should be 'clicking' either. Surely they go 'diddly dum diddly dee, diddly dum diddly dee', don't they?

- Individuals reported that pet tortoises had been stolen.

Hang on! This one's all right, isn't it? That would be theft, and theft is illegal, yeah?

So how would you classify a valid 999 call? Here you go ...

WALTHAM FOREST POLICE APPEAL: CALL 999 TO REPORT SQUIRREL DROWNINGS

www.thisislocallondon.co.uk

Allotment holders who trap and drown squirrels are being targeted by police – and officers are even urging people to call 999 if they witness them doing it.

So squirrel drowning = emergency, while tortoise theft = inappropriate? Double standards at work here ...

Hang on a minute! || PAUSE, << REWIND, ▶ PLAY. People are drowning squirrels?

Call 999 or ... burn the murdering swines' sheds down! Pour petrol on their outbuildings and torch them! (Okay, that's just my suggestion, not the police.)

43

Drowning mammals is a criminal offence under the Wild Mammals Protection Act 1996.

There's a 'drowning mammals' law? Every credit, but just mammals? Very discriminatory that, isn't it? What about birds and reptiles?

Sgt Rowan Healey, borough wildlife crime officer, said ...

They have a borough wildlife crime officer? I know they live in the forest of Waltham, but how widespread is wildlife crime? Does every borough have one?

... 'There is clearly a misunderstanding here because anybody advising others to drown squirrels is encouraging them to break the law.

'Incitement to drown a squirrel.' Hanging's too good for 'em.

'There are organizations that can give advice on ways to discourage squirrels ...

Pinch their nuts ... if you can get near enough.

'... without harming them.'

Ah, scratch that, then.

It is not believed that any squirrels have been found drowned.
∎

What?! (Does double take.) What, none?

So, very confused now. Referring back to the report's opening paragraph: 'Allotment holders who trap and drown squirrels are being targeted by police.' Yet actually 'it is not believed that any squirrels have been found drowned'. And these are the same police who haven't got time to look for stolen tortoises? What a sad waste of police resources.

I have this lingering thought that Sgt Rowan Healey – you know, the 'borough wildlife crime officer' – might possibly have exaggerated the facts to get his crime stats up and justify his rather dubious post.

Man sentenced after claiming to have been raped by a wombat

The Age

Arthur Ross Cradock, a 48-year-old orchard worker, admitted in the Nelson District Court yesterday to the charge of using a phone for a fictitious purpose ...

... after calling police with the message: 'I've been raped by a wombat.'

And I say to myself, what a wonderful world.

What sort of law is that?! 'Using a phone for a fictitious purpose' – that's brilliant.

Can you imagine being the police officer who took that call?

Scene: Police Call Centre

Police Officer:
I'm sorry, it's a bad line, it sounds like you're saying that you were raped by a wombat. Do you mean a woman with a bat? No? Chased by a wildcat? (Pause.) So, right first time, then ... raped by a wombat ... gotcha!

By the way, does anybody remember Willy Wombat? I reckon it was him.

What did Mr Cradock expect the police to do? Come out, take a statement, question suspects? Show him mugshots of wombats with a history of sexual assault, sort out an identity parade? What?

He called the police again soon after and gave his full name, saying he wanted to withdraw the complaint. 'I'll retract the rape complaint from the wombat, because he's pulled out,' Cradock told the operator.

He's pulled out?! So when he phoned the first time, the wombat was still raping him, but now he's pulled out? 'Hang on to the wombat till we get there, Mr Cradock!'

'Apart from speaking Australian now, I'm pretty all right, you know, I didn't hurt my bum at all,' Cradock told the operator.

It is a little-known side effect of wombat sex that it can result in you speaking Australian. And when I say speaking Australian, I obviously mean speaking English, but adding an upward intonation at the end of every sentence as if it's a question. Practise now: 'I was raped by a wom*bat*?'

That's how it starts.

Whoa! That's a hell of a bet! He lost his money, wife, health *and* livelihood? That's a Yankee, that is. Six doubles, four trebles and an accumulator.

The 28-year-old greyhound trainer of Sedgeletch Road ...

... claims the bookmakers allowed him to carry on betting after he asked them to stop taking his money under the company's own self-exclusion policy.

■

So he didn't lose his house, then – thank heavens for small mercies. If he'd have bet that as well, it would have been a Heinz 57 super bet.

'I'll have five grand on "Lame Boy" in the 7.15 at Hackney. No, hang on! Please don't take it, please. Oh, you've taken it!'

Just for this one story, I'm going to give you the headline at the end.

Lancashire Evening Post

Twenty teachers chase an escaped beast in 30-minute playground mayhem.

An escaped 'beast' in a playground? For half an hour? That's proper mayhem, that is.

Screaming youngsters scattered in fear when an escaped llama ran amok ...

Whoa, steady on! A llama? You know when they said 'beast'? 'Llama' was way down my list – below 'goat', as it happens, and that was in the bottom half.

When you say 'beast' in this country, you first imagine a wildcat of some kind, or a wild boar, or a mad, nasty badger.

(I hit a badger once. In a car, I mean – I'm not daft enough to actually punch one because they are vicious and even if you landed a decent combination the chances are that it wouldn't feel it and it would still have your arm off.)

Around twenty teachers ...

So I'm guessing nineteen or twenty-one?

... spent half an hour chasing the rampaging farm animal.

Brave maths teacher Karl Lomax grabbed the animal in a bear hug ...

... while language tutor Anne Woodcock lasooed [sic] it with a rope.

The llama then decided to sit down until it was reunited with its owner.

■

That's more like it – not so much a 'beast', more a 'farm animal'.

By coincidence, I had a maths teacher who was a beast.

It doesn't specify which language Miss Woodcock teaches – but an English teacher would have *lassoed* it.

Llamas know when the game's up.

And *now* for the headline:

LLAMA DRAMA DING DONG

Take a bow, Phil Gorner at the *Lancashire Evening Post*. Absolute genius. I bet he wrote that and then took the rest of the week off.

STRIMMER KING PLANS TO BE A ROCKET MAN

The Bolton News

A fearless inventor is set to forsake his garden-strimmer-powered pushbike for a rocket machine.

A Bolton man plans to adapt the same old faithful bike into a real velocipede and compete in a standing start sprint against the stopwatch. He said, 'I haven't spoken to any rocket manufacturers yet about it.'

■

Where exactly is 'Strimmer'? Is it a monarchy and does it have a space programme?

Ah, so not the King of Strimmer? Not a king at all. Just a bloke who has a strimmer-powered pushbike (so technically not a pushbike).

He's going to fit a rocket to a bike? I've got to see that. On your marks, get set, go! Vrooom ...

Er, anyone seen Bill? You know Bill — he's a 'fearless inventor' or, as we like to call him, idiot.

Council refuses to clean up spilt bin without staff qualified to wear wellies

Daily Telegraph

Yes, you read it right.

Cllr Barnard, the vice-chairman of Harting Parish Council in West Sussex, contacted his local authority after receiving complaints that an old metal bin had fallen into a stream. It was pouring out rubbish including dog faeces at the end of the footpath where mothers and children walk to school.

How did he know it was dog faeces?

He said, 'I spoke to someone from the department dealing with fly-tipping and he said – and I quote – "We don't have anyone qualified to wear wellington boots."

You've got to admit that it's a brilliant top-of-the-head excuse.

'I said, "But it's only four inches deep."

'Then he said that the problem was that they also needed harnesses and ropes to stop them getting washed away.'
■

I bet that took the wind out of his sails.

Exactly which council is this? Lilliput?

BOYS KICKED OUT OF SCHOOL FOR TAKING VIAGRA

Daily Record

Two 14-year-old boys were caught taking Viagra in school. Police are investigating after the second-year pupils were hauled before the headmaster.

A source at the school said: 'They were pulled into the headmaster's office.

'Hauled', eh? Excellent verb in the circumstances.

First 'hauled' and now 'pulled'! Even better. I'd love to have seen them 'pulled' into his office: 'Come along with me, young man' (grabs obvious erection and drags him into the office).

'The boys have claimed not to have taken any of [the drugs], but there has been good reason to believe that was not the case.'

GP Craig Lennox said, 'The most likely thing that would happen to someone who took too much is a prolonged and painful erection.'

■

Yeah, especially when one of them tripped, fell over and pole-vaulted into the staff room! 'There has been good reason to believe that was not the case.' Makes you smile, doesn't it?

What benefit did these lads think that taking Viagra would have? When you're fourteen, you live your life with a prolonged and painful erection. Starts first thing in the morning on the way to school with the bus's engine throbbing away. (There is a medical term for this – it's called 'diesel dick' and side effects include standing up too soon at your stop and having a pensioner's eye out.)

So ... Viagra

I read recently that, in certain individuals, Viagra can cause blindness. So your mum was right, wasn't she? It attacks the retina of the eye and causes a syndrome called blue vision, which can lead to blindness. This is obviously a terrible side effect for a couple of reasons. One, you go blind – obviously bad enough; but two, you've popped a Viagra because you're on a promise and now you're staggering around the bedroom with a stiffy going, 'Am I getting warm?' 'No, but you're scaring the dog! Go left.'

Believe it or not, I'm still too young to qualify for Viagra. I do fancy having a go, though. I went to the chemist and asked if I could get it over the counter, and he said, 'If you take two, there's a chance.'

In India, it is prescribed for patients with severe sunburn in combination with calamine lotion. The calamine soothes the burns while the Viagra keep the covers off them.

I've tried natural alternatives – oysters, ginseng, horny goat weed. I tried celery once, but that was more of a splint (here's a tip, chop the leaves off: the ladies don't like them).

My wife read something in a magazine about powdered rhinoceros horn (or, as she called it, 'African Disiac') and she sent me to one of these holistic practitioners to get some. I asked about side effects and he told me that they were rare except that now and again I might want to head-butt a Land Rover. So I went home with it and as soon as I walked in the door, I knew it was going to be put to the test.

In the bedroom, my wife said, 'Tie me to the bed!' So I did. 'Now do anything you want ... anything.' So I had a wash and a shave and went for a pint ...

Anyway, long story short, the powdered rhino horn worked. She put some in my bedtime drink – but doubled the dose and I went straight to sleep. When I woke up the next morning, she was the Ice Maiden. Wouldn't speak to me, wouldn't look at me, totally cold. But THEN!

At about half past ten, she was bending over getting something out of the chest freezer and the red mist descended and my temples started to throb (and they weren't the only thing) as the rhino horn kicked in big time and – without a second thought – I hopped on. Mounted her there and then and gave her a proper good seeing-to. When it was over, I thought she'd be thrilled to bits, but now we've been banned from Tesco, so ...

Irish traveller's behaviour 'a disgrace'

www.news.com.au

An Irish traveller has been sent home in disgrace after committing a series of bizarre crimes while drunk. Richard William O'Flynn, 25, was at the end of a two-year working holiday visa when he embarked on the unusual crime spree in Brisbane late last year, the Brisbane District Court was told today.

Okay, we've established they were 'bizarre' and 'unusual' crimes – come on, what did he do?

His most bizarre act was to take a goldfish into a Ticketek office in the CBD and demand money so he could pay for food to feed it, the court was told.

Wait a minute – 'I need money to feed my goldfish' is actually brilliant, bordering on genius. And yes, I grant you, it *is* bizarre, but surely not a crime?

59

On another occasion, he and a male friend got drunk and entered a cake store where he demanded a 'gay cake' for their 'gay wedding'.

You've gotta love him, haven't you? And again, where's the crime? All cakes are a bit gay, aren't they? Or was it 'demanding a cake with menaces'?

O'Flynn then picked up a cake-decorating knife and threatened the assistant, asking for money.

Ah, Richard! See what you've done now? You've let yourself down, you've let your family down, you've let your friends down and, more importantly, you've let your country down. Threatening behaviour with a 'cake-decorating knife'? You'll never forgive yourself. I bet the assistant wasn't intimidated, was she?

When the assistant told him she would call the police, he and his friend left the store, the court was told.

See, he didn't mean any harm, did he?

Scene: 'Cake That' Cake Store

Shop Assistant:
Behave or I'll call the police.

O'Flynn:
Oh right, sure, we'll be going then.

O'Flynn pleaded guilty to one count each of attempted armed robbery and attempted stealing.

Attempted armed robbery? Hardly.

He also pleaded guilty to using a carriage service to menace ...

Don't ask me, it's an Australian thing.

... harass or cause offence ...

Make your mind up: menace, harass or cause offence – which?

... after repeatedly calling an estate agent and abusing her because she left a flyer in his mailbox.

It's an estate agent so ... I'd say none of the above. I'd say guilty to 'pestering a bit'.

O'Flynn, who will return to Ireland at the end of the month, also pleaded guilty to wilful damage for kicking a car during an argument in Bundaberg. Judge Milton Griffin sentenced him to 12 months' jail suspended after 80 days, which he had already served in pre-sentence custody. Judge Griffin described O'Flynn's behaviour as 'disgraceful' ...

You say 'disgraceful', I say 'hilarious' – well, apart from the car kicking.

... and said that Australia would be better off without him. 'We will all be altogether pleased to see you go,' Judge Griffin said.

■

'All be altogether pleased'?! That's rubbish English. And by the way, Judge Griffin, you've played right into Mr O'Flynn's hands. He's caught you hook, line and sinker with his ingenious plan. He's got to the end of his two-year working holiday visa and he's not got any money to get him home to Ireland, so he concocts a plan to commit a series of bizarre crimes and get deported. Nobody got hurt, nobody suffered any real harm and he's on his way home. Good times.

I do have a worry about what's happened to his goldfish. I hope his 'gay' friend is looking after it, feeding it the occasional slice of 'gay cake' off the cake-decorating knife ...

Denbighshire Visitor

LLANGOLLEN **students from 17 of the town's schools** swapped sandwiches for sushi during their recent transition week as part of a celebration of Japanese culture.

Over 200 Year 6 pupils from feeder primary schools around the town ...

That'd be whale, then.* Eating whale in Wales? That somehow seems so wrong.

You say, 'Sushi'; I say, 'Orca.'

Plenty to feed on here, kids. You can make a whale go a long way; further than turkey at Christmas, even. (Do they eat turkey in Turkey?)

* See page 65.

... have spent their week in Ysgol Dinas Brân learning about the land of the rising sun, following on from a visit by Japanese students to the school last year.

'It is a great opportunity for pupils from different years to work together and share their experience to help each other,' said Mark Hatch, Assistant Headteacher. 'The Africa week last year played a huge part in helping pupils settle here in September.'

■

I don't follow. Am I being dim? How did it help pupils settle there? How big is the Ysgol Dinas Brân's catchment area – because I'm telling you now that, even accepting that getting your kids into school is a bit of a lottery these days, I'd be a bit mad if my kid lived down the road and he couldn't get in, but half a dozen six-year-olds from Lagos did. Apart from anything else, it's so impractical! Think of the travelling.

* The official line, of course, is that Japan only hunts whales for scientific research. Yeah, right – like which whale tastes nicer, blue whale or minky whale? Which makes the nicest pie? Which makes the tastiest burger? (Oh yes, they have whale burgers in Japan – that's what I call a whopper.)

Japanese scientists say that whales need culling because they are depleting the world's fish stocks. What, more than we are with our enormous factory ships? How many fish does a whale eat? How much do we eat?

They also say that the whales are killed humanely. Well, Mr Japanese Scientist, how about I shoot you with an explosive crossbow bolt, then drag you round the house for an hour and a half, and then drown you in the bath?

Mind you, it's not just Japan, is it? Norway are at it again, so I'm calling for a boycott of all Norwegian goods, like … er… Christmas trees, for a start.

Christmas tree axed

Buxton Advertiser

Chinley's village Christmas tree will no longer be situated on Squirrel Green.

Because of vandalism, Chinley, Buxworth and Brownside Parish Council will instead provide a smaller tree in the window of their Parish Room. Councillor Trefor Jones said, 'The tree will still be in the centre of the village, but at least the vandals would not be able to get hold of it.

'This seems to be a logical solution.'

Someone chopped the Christmas tree down? I suspect Greenpeace.

Oh no. It's just a dramatic headline for this story.

Squirrel Green in Chinley? Is this the next village to Trumpton?

Wanna bet? Oh, and by the way, shocking grammar.

Define 'logical', Cllr Jones. This is completely illogical. Who voted for this idiot?

1) You think putting the tree behind a window – a glass window – and announcing in the press that it will deter vandals will actually deter vandals? Vandals love windows.

2) Every house in Chinley will probably have a Christmas tree in the window. Why would anyone consider that this tree was the Village Tree?

3) Why should the squirrels on Squirrel Green be denied their Christmas tree … or was it the squirrels doing the damage? Ripping the baubles off and throwing them at each other. Pesky squirrels.

The logical solution would have been to leave it in the usual place, but booby-trap it: a couple of mantraps (sorry, person-traps) and exposed electrical wiring. Job done.

Now TWO stories from the *same edition* of the *Derbyshire Times* ...

FREEZE PUTS SQUEEZE ON BUDGET

Nice rhyming there, *Derbyshire Times*.

Keeping Derbyshire's roads free from ice and snow this winter has blown the county council's budget by more than £2m. The prolonged cold weather has meant that roads had to be gritted more often than expected.

I wish I'd put my money in grit rather than the Northern Rock. I'd have made a fortune this past winter if I'd invested in a grit mountain.

An extra £35 a tonne! How many tonnes in a grit mountain?!

What a missed opportunity … especially when you consider that it wasn't just Derbyshire that had extra demand for grit, it was the whole country. Grit was like gold dust – well, not exactly like it; it's sort of brown coloured and a bit rougher, grittier, you might say, than actual dust, but you get my drift.

It was in such short supply that people were emptying supermarket shelves of cat litter and using that to de-ice their roads and paths. That's mad. I can't follow the thought process there. Were they so long-sighted that they thought it said 'Gritter' on the packet not 'Litter', or did they think that because it looks exactly the same (there are similarities) it would act in the same way? D'oh!

Needless to say, it didn't work and simply resulted in a nation of confused cats going to the toilet on the highways and byways – and slipping on their backsides as they did so.

The short supplies resulted in roads not on the precautionary salting network – which includes around half of the county's roads – only being treated on an emergency basis.

Someone's going to break their neck out there and then where will we be?

ABUSIVE BEHAVIOUR

A boozy man ...

... ejected from a pub after midnight kicked out when police tried to arrest him, a court heard.

The landlady of The Angel at Clowne called police and asked them to remove Drew Whitehead during the early hours of February 7. Whitehead (24) ran away, but fell on icy ground ...

Is that an acceptable adjective? Or does he come from a place called 'Boozy'? Not likely, is it?

Kicked out then kicked out, as surely as night follows day ...

Now, if The Angel at Clowne was on the precautionary salting network, he'd have got away, so ... every cloud has a silver lining.

Mind you, I wouldn't grit a place called 'Clowne' anyway, would you? You'd want to see everybody slipping and sliding about on their really big shoes, wouldn't you?

... and then kicked out while shouting and swearing at officers.

He was put inside a police van and he banged his head on windows inside the vehicle.

I couldn't be a policeman. I'd find it difficult to exercise restraint while being abused like that.

Oops-a-daisy. Accidents will happen, your honour.

Cow shot dead following police chase

CANWEST NEWS SERVICE

What started as a seemingly light-hearted story of cattle roaming through a neighbourhood Thursday morning quickly turned deadly serious after a police officer fired more than a dozen shots and killed one of the animals.

The incident started after a pickup truck hauling four cattle rolled over during the morning rush hour. Police constable Dave Woodford said, 'They were running up and down Queen Elizabeth Way and were smart enough to get off at Dixie Road so they didn't get hit by any cars.'

He fired more than a dozen shots? Someone needs a little more time on the firing range ...

Cows are smarter than we give them credit for. (See page 76.)

He said, 'We were following this cow and all of a sudden it turned and started charging at the officer.

So mooooove, it's a cow, they're not that agile. Just step to one side and watch it go sliding past. Turn on to Dixie Road, you numpty. That's what the cows did. And they're the ones who are supposed to be dumb.

'He just pulled his handgun out and started shooting at it.

Oh well done, officer, good move. After all, you are dealing with a cow — one of nature's most efficient killing machines. Eat you as soon as look at you, cows would.

'It would be like a car coming at you, that's what it would be like.

What? Behave! A car would be (a) much faster and (b) I'm guessing quite a bit wider. But even so, let's not forget it still took him more than a dozen shots to down it. Here's a tip, officer — Specsavers, two for one.

'We looked at the safety of people and the safety of the officers at the time and we weren't prepared to shoot it.

Yes, you were. You had guns — amply prepared, I'd say.

'That wasn't in our plan.'

What was your plan? There's no mention of a plan ...

Go on. What was your plan?

You didn't have one, did you? So you just blasted it.

> Woodford wasn't sure where the cattle were being taken ...
>
> ... but said it might have been the slaughterhouse.

I don't want to try to teach my granny how to suck eggs, but you know what I'd have done? I'd have asked the driver.

'Might have been'? Where else? The zoo, or the pictures, or ten-pin bowling or – I know! – yachting round the Isle of Wight?

So ... Cows

I think cows are smart and misunderstood. They have many talents, the greatest of which is weather forecasting. We humans have developed billions of pounds worth of hardware and software on earth and out in space, all programmed to forecast weather patterns, and it's hardly ever right. Ever! Total waste of time, money and effort. On the weather forecast this morning, some woman announced that there was a 50 per cent chance of rain. So thanks for that! Really helpful. I'll consult with the cows, thank you very much.

Because we know from our childhood that cows know ages before we do that it's going to rain. Travelling with our parents to the seaside, we'd peer out of car, bus or train windows and our mum would say, 'Oh no, it's going to rain!' 'How do you know?' we'd ask. 'The cows are lying down.'

And for years I thought that it wasn't a bad life being a cow. Wandering round a field all day, chewing the cud, making a cowpat and predicting rain. I don't know if cows are competitive, whether some are better at sensing rain than others, but I have a feeling they might be. Wandering round the field, keeping an eye on the elements and one moos, 'Rain coming! Rain coming!' But just as they all start to go down, another one moos, 'No! Bit of blue sky!' And most save themselves, but for the odd one it's too late, they've fully committed and the others moo sarcastically, 'Daisy, get up, you fool, bit of blue sky, are you blind?'

Years later, I think that cows' weather-forecasting skills are more extensive than we understand. I think we've latched onto the lying down–rain indicator, but I think they exhibit other behavioural activities for other weather. For sun, I think they give a little happy jump now and again. For windy conditions approaching, I think they sway about a bit.

Sheep are no good at it. They look over the fence from the adjoining field, observing this behaviour, and ask each other, 'What are they doing? They're mad, that lot.' And the sad thing, the really sad thing, is that we do the same.

Mind you, I was nearly killed by a cow once. Staggering home cross-country, drunk as a skunk, I lay down in a field and went to sleep. Minutes later, I woke to see a cow bearing down on me – but I was lucky, it just grazed me.

Sorry.

But on a slightly different tack, my gran had a friend who had her own weather-forecasting method. She told my gran that when she woke up in the morning on a washing day, she would pull the bedclothes back and look at her husband's willy. If it was lying to the right, it was going to rain, so she would hang her wet clothes up in the kitchen. If it was lying to the left, it was going to be fine, so she could hang them outside. My gran asked, cheekily, what would happen if it was 'standing up' and her friend replied, 'I don't do any washing.'

COOP PERMISSION IS SET TO RUN OUT

Leamington Spa Courier

A year after its controversial unveiling, Leamington's much-maligned pigeon coop could soon meet its end.

Temporary planning permission on the 48-box structure runs out at the end of this month. Old Town regenerate group Regenesis . . .

Oh! Pigeon coop! I thought it meant the Co-op.

Sounds like a Phil Collins tribute band.

... used £13,500 of taxpayers' money to erect the coop on Court Street and billed it as a five-star home as well as being the second part of a pigeon management scheme which had already seen signs put up at pigeon-feeding hot spots around town calling on people to stop.

All sounds good. Congratulations all round, but only a 48-box structure? Will that be enough for Leamington's pigeon population?

After six months, the 'no feeding' signs had made little impact and the big white box still had no residents.

More than enough, obviously.

It was only when birds were forcibly captured and netted in that the coop started to fulfil its brief ...

Hang on! They started forcibly catching pigeons and chucking them in the coop? Surely that's not the answer?

... amid allegations of animal cruelty by pigeon experts.

If there are pigeon experts in Leamington, I probably would have involved them in the coop's management earlier.

Even today it seems the coop is still virtually unused. Coop manager Janet Alty was unavailable for comment.

I'd be tempted to give Bill Oddie a ring.

Felines are making our lives a misery

Warrington Guardian

A family claim they are being hounded by a bunch of cats.

The family say that if they had been plagued by dogs, then something would have been done.

'If my dog was wandering the streets, I would be for the high jump.'

The cats also interrupt the family's sleep as they hang around outside the windows.

Cats, then?

Maybe not cats then, if 'hounded'. Cats don't hound ... do they? Cats, er ... prowl? Stalk?

Hang on, 'plagued', that's rats. Maybe that's it, easy mistake to make: cats – rats.

Correct, because in Warrington, your dog wandering the streets is an Olympic-qualifying event.

I'd love to see that. Opening the curtains and being confronted by half a dozen cats hanging from the window frame staring in, smiling.

> 'There's a cats' chorus outside because they are all in high spirits at this time of the year.'
> ■

'High spirits'! That's cats for you. But actually that's funnier, opening your curtains and there's a gang of cats hanging from your window frame, singing like a barbershop quartet because they are in such high spirits.

What would a cats' chorus sing? 'Catanooga Choo Choo'? 'It's Got to Be Purrfect'? 'Goodness Gracious Fur Balls of Fire'?

Dad's got write stuff

Oldham Advertiser

Doting dad Adam Perrot has decided that he's had enough of selling books and is going to write them himself. This year the father of one has decided to divert all his energy to his true calling while also being a stay-at-home dad to his seven-month-old son Caleb.

I'd not divert *all* your energy to your true calling, mate, I have a feeling you'll need quite a bit for Caleb.

By the way – Caleb? Whatever happened to James, John, David? I just happen to know that Caleb's name is very similar to the Hebrew word '*kéleb*' meaning 'dog', which in the past has led to the common misconception that the name 'Caleb' actually means 'dog', but as we all know, Caleb was the son of Jephunneh, an important figure in the Hebrew Bible, noted for his religious faith when the Hebrews point-blank refused to enter the 'promised land' of Canaan.

Remember that? Yes, you do. You know, when the Hebrews came to the outskirts of Canaan, and Moses (the Hebrew top '*kéleb*') sent forth twelve spies to report back on what lay ahead. Ten of the scouts advised that the land would be impossible to claim; that giants lived there who would defeat the Hebrew army. Just two, Joshua (from the tribe of Ephraim) and Caleb (representing Judah), decreed that God would be able to deliver Canaan to them.

Of course, we all know what happened next. The Bible records that, due to the testimony of the ten scouts, the Hebrews decided not to enter Canaan. As punishment for this flagrant disobedience, God caused them to wander in the desert for forty years before they were finally permitted to conquer Canaan as their home. (So much for democracy, eh? Ten against two and God gets the hump, really ticked off!)

Just two adults were permitted to survive these forty years and enter the promised land: Joshua and Caleb, as a reward for their faith in God. And so, it's the ideal name for a kid from Oldham.

Adam will be leaving the town centre store – now owned by Waterstones – next month. He explained, 'I've been working at the bookshop for six and a half years and have been writing for six of those years. I've been through two takeovers at the shop and have received millions of rejection letters for my work …

'Millions of rejection letters'?! *Millions*?! That, my friend, is one huge unanimous rejection. Without getting the *Yellow Pages* out, I'm guessing that this is nearly every publisher in, let's see, The World. Are you sure this is your true calling, Adam? Because 'millions' of people can't be wrong, mate – your writing must stink.

' … but now I'll use the time I'll not be spending with Caleb.'

You'll be with him all the time! That's top of the job description for stay-at-home dads.

His passion for literature has already rubbed off on his son, who is most comfortable with his nose stuck in a book.

No way! He's seven months old. He can't be comfortable like that, get him a pillow.

Adam said, 'We got him his first book before he was born and he now knows how to turn the pages and things.'

'And *things*'? Adam, as a writer, you're going to have to do better than that. 'And ... *what*?' What are those 'things'? Imagination and descriptive skills seem sadly lacking. Add that to the 'millions' of rejections and ask yourself a question – is it too late to withdraw your resignation?

REGISTRAR TO MARRY HER OWN SISTER

News & Star, Carlisle

A registrar will put the 'law' into 'brother-in-law' today. Superintendent registrar Sue Oliver will be marrying her sister Jayne Jones and her fiancé David Moffat at Penrith register office.

Surely that's not allowed?!
Not even in Carlisle ...

Ah, I see ... but that's not what the headline suggests, is it?

Nine families with same name make for postal chaos

Irish Independent

By Anita Guidera

A rural community is devising its own system to help the postman distinguish between nine families that share the same surname.

In the small Donegal townland of Ballinacor near Crossroads, Killygordon ...

... live nine Carlin families, including four men called John Carlin. Finally reaching the end of his tether after receiving a bill which was not for him, John J Carlin ...

Sing, 'Postal chaos, postal chaos – go together like a horse and carriage. It's an institute you can't disparage ...'

Well, actually you can, most of the time.

Nine families in the same village with the same surname? Gimme a high six!

Ah, twinned with Insest, South Carolina.

They've got him tethered?! That's a bit medieval, isn't it – albeit understandable if he's the man responsible for all the little Carlins knocking about.

... approached the local community group, Crossroads and Killygordon Enterprise ...

... to ask if they could find a solution to the Carlin problem.

The CAKE committee ...

That's 'CAKE'! A community CAKE! Hang on a minute. Let me check the date of this report ... Nope, not 1 April. CAKE! I wonder if someone proposed Crossroads and Killygordon Association? CAKA instead of CAKE would have made for a difficult decision.

How do you solve a problem like John Carlin? It will have to be something so ingenious ...

Technically – CAKECOM.

Scene: Operations Room, CAKECOM

CAKE Chairperson *(let's call him 'Eccles'):*
How do we solve the 'Carlin' problem?

CAKE Member 1 *(let's call her 'Battenberg'):*
It's a dilemma layered on a conundrum with a puzzle topping.

CAKE Member 2 *(let's call him Charlie):*
I propose we go to CAKECOM 1.

CAKE Member 3 *(let's call her 'Angel'):*
No, it's too early! We need to consult.

Eccles:
What do you think, Cream?

CAKE Member 4 *(Cream):*
I don't know! I'm stuck somewhere in the middle …

Eccles:
Jam?

CAKE Member 5 *(Jam):*
I'm with Cream on this one.

… is now working on a system to ensure that each house in the townland will have its own unique number.

What?! But that's genius! Thank God for CAKECOM. They're going to give the houses a number, and even better a unique number, so that no two houses will have the same number! Sounds great on paper, but will it work?

A similar project has been pioneered by the nearby Meenreagh Development Association …

MDA? That's mad! Well, not quite 'mad', it's an anagram of 'mad', but in any case, it's not as good as CAKE, is it?

I'm going to write to see if they'll change it to Meenreagh Urban Development, so 'MUD'.

You know when people say, 'Their name's mud around here'? Well, that could be their slogan.

... where most of its residents shared the Gallen surname.

They need to adopt Ballinacor's tethering policy.

John Carlin explained the confusion in Ballinacor, which has become a great annoyance to the four Johns, including John 'the rate' Carlin, his grandson Johnny, his neighbour and of course John J himself. 'I used to be the only John Carlin in the townland ...

'The only John Carlin in the townland': I think it's been done. But who was first, that's the question.

'... now the place is full of them.

'Full of them'? Steady on, John J, there's four. The townland can't be full, surely. How many people live in Ballinacor?

'It's terrible, especially when a new postman comes on the route. The whole thing goes haywire.'

The whole thing? What whole thing? The CAKE-whole thing?

89

He said that the situation came to a head recently when a large bill arrived in the post from a local company which supplies home heating oil. But John is a stick and turf man and doesn't even have an oil tank.

You wouldn't have an oil tank if you were a stick and turf man, would you? That would be a pointless and expensive exercise. What you'd want is a big stick store.

'A similar numbering system was done very successfully in Meenreagh where there was a similar problem,' he added.

Hang on, though, John J. I think you're blowing this problem out of all proportion. After all, we've established that there's only three other John Carlins in town. I'm assuming that you know what type of heating your neighbour and grandson Johnny use, so if it's not them, I'd pop round to John 'the rate' Carlin's house, it can't be far away, and give him the bill.

'And I don't care what number I get on my door, any number will do for me.'

A spokesman for An Post said that he was unaware of any similar scheme being promoted by a community group in Ireland. 'There is no such scheme that An Post is aware of, but we will certainly co-operate with any community group who wishes to put numbers or names on houses, as this would help speed up our operation,' the spokesman said.

∎

You don't need numbers on doors! There are only four Johns in the townland, right? There's you – John J Carlin; your grandson, Johnny Carlin; John 'the rate' Carlin; and plain John Carlin the neighbour. You've all got different names! And if you can't figure out how to use that in your address, here's a tip – number the John Carlins, rather than disrupt the whole townland. So the oldest becomes John Carlin 1 and the youngest John Carlin 4. After all, it's a bit radical putting numbers on houses. What will the post office (An Post) think of that?

I must just check the date of this article again ... No, it is definitely 2008.

CHEF TAKES THE BISCUIT

Evening Chronicle, Newcastle

Freaky eater Andrew Foster had a phobia of meat, fish and vegetables and could not taste food he cooked in his restaurant.

He's a chef?! How did that happen? He must have had the stupidest careers officer on the planet. Who would eat in a restaurant where the chef couldn't taste the food?

So basically he's had a fear of meat, fish and veg since when?

'When I was 18 months old I stopped eating.

Why aren't you dead then?

'Experts advised my mum to starve me ...

Ha, ha, ha ... that's what she told you they'd said! And, by the way, I don't think they were real experts. 'Starve him!' they said.

'... as I'd eventually eat. But the only thing I'd want was biscuits.'

Now, with the help of a psychologist . . .

Scene: Psychologist's Office

Psychologist:
Crackers.

Andrew:
I love 'em.

Psychologist:
No, mate, I mean you're *crackers.*

.... and a nutritionist, he's been taught a distraction technique to help him try new foods.

It'll probably be that one where your mum puts some food on a spoon and 'flies' it around in front of your face, making a humming noise that's supposed to sound like an aeroplane, before zooming directly at your mouth, which you open as the plane flies in. Although I don't know what sort of a pilot would fly into a gaping chasm ...

Andrew has since discovered the delights of meat, fish, fruit and a host of vegetables, saving biscuits as a treat. He said, 'It's like a whole new world and now I'm able to taste my recipes — making them even better!'

Well, yeah. I can see how tasting them might help. And now they're even better? Surprise, that.

The *Evening Chronicle* helpfully illustrates the story with a feature.

Andrew's average daily menu consists of:

Breakfast – Large glass of milk and biscuits.

Lunch – Crisps, fizzy drinks and six or seven ...

Wanna guess?

... biscuits.

Correct!

Dinner ...

Guess again?

... Toast.

Wrong!

Mother's fine for dropping sausage roll makes no sense

Hull Daily Mail

As first reported in the *Mail*, Sarah Davies was trying to put a bite-sized piece of pastry into her four-year-old daughter Chloe's mouth ...

... but misjudged it and it fell on the ground.

Two Hull City Council officials immediately stopped Miss Davies, 20, and told her she would be given a fixed penalty notice.

Just pastry, note. Kept the savoury filling for herself.

How can you miss a four-year-old's mouth with a bite-sized piece of pastry? They're like ravenous cuckoos.

Just plain bad luck that two council officials were passing instead of local MP John Prescott. If he'd have been there, that bite-sized piece of pastry would never have hit the ground.

A council spokeswoman said, 'While we are unable to discuss the individual details of the case, we would like to stress the information reported in the *Mail* is not an accurate account of the incident.' The council refuses to state what part of the story – as described by Miss Davies – was not accurate.

I have some sympathy for the council here, for there is an element of doubt, mi'lud. For a start, the article is accompanied by a picture of Sarah Davies carrying four-year-old Chloe (who, by the way, is nearly as big as her mum), under which is the caption: 'Sarah Davies was given a £75 fixed penalty after her daughter Chloe dropped a piece of sausage roll on the ground in Hull.'

So, who did drop the piece of sausage roll? Mum or Chloe? The stories don't match up. Wouldn't stand up in court.

In any case, you probably think like I do. One of them dropped the piece of pastry and couldn't be arsed picking it up. And that's littering.

Shoe store raiders walk off with safe

Derbyshire Times

A safe was stolen and cash was taken from a till of an Alfreton shop. The break-in, through a rear door, happened at Shoe Zone on the High Street.

■

A safe and cash from a till at Shoe Zone? It doesn't say how much they got away with, but if it was a full day's takings it could amount to nearly three figures.

THIEVES MAKE OFF WITH £12,000 OF BULL SEMEN FROM SCOTS FARM

Daily Record

The theft took place near Brydekirk, Dumfriesshire some time between Sunday and Thursday.

Somebody left a pile of bull semen (maybe not 'pile' – I'm not sure how it's stored; probably not in a pile, actually) unattended for five days?!

The semen is stored in a special flask containing liquid nitrogen to keep it at a fixed temperature.

So, like a Thermos?

A police spokesman said some form of transport must have been used in the raid as the flask weighed 66 lbs.

That is a load of bull.

He said, 'Due to the high value, it will have a market – somebody will take it off their hands.'

■

Urgh – there's got to be a better way of dispensing it.

NB: I read recently that there are 50 million spermatozoa in one teaspoon of sperm. I thought, 'It's the twenty-first century, there's got to be a more scientific method of measuring sperm than using cutlery. Does Brussels know about this?'

The same article said that human sperm is ejaculated at 28 mph – that's quick! I wonder who measured that? Did some Biology undergraduate base his thesis on the speed of sperm? Did he/she modify one of those police speed guns? Call it a 'seed gun' and go to a volunteer … 'Now!' – 'Ahhhh' – Beep – '28 mph!'

Anyway – back to the missing Dumfriesshire sperm. Any news?

My new hair-moo

Daily Record (again)

Customers at an upmarket hair salon are being offered a new treatment for split ends — bull semen.

The organic Angus sperm combined with plant roots is said to do wonders for dry, coarse hair.

Hairdresser Hari Salem ...

... said, 'It is a very unusual treatment, but the sperm is very nourishing.'

■

Excellent.

Sperm is great for split ends? Let me just make a note of that.

Okay, readers, I know you're saying rip-off; I'm saying ammunition for marital discussion. So let me write this down: 'is said to do wonders for dry, coarse hair ...'

A whole new meaning for Salem's Lot.

Oh what?! God bless you, Mr Salem. That's the clincher! 'Sperm is very nourishing', it's great for split ends and it does 'wonders for dry, coarse hair'. I thank you. Wait till I get home.

UNFORESEEN MISHAP

The Times

An astrology enthusiast set fire to her house with a crystal ball.

Margaret Padwick, who is in her seventies, left the ball on a window ledge and while she was out, it reflected the sun onto her curtains.

She returned to her home in Poole, Dorset to find her lounge full of smoke.

Dave Cooper of Dorset Fire Service said, 'It was most unusual.

'The conditions were just right with a low, strong October sun.'

I know it's tempting, but don't say anything yet.

Try to keep it to yourself.

Just a little longer.

Really? Not a regular occurrence round your way, then?

Oh, I see. That's what was unusual. Loads of people leave crystal balls on their window ledges, it's just that in this case ...

Okay, dear reader, you can say it now – it's time for the tag line. Altogether ... Surely she must have seen that coming! Oh yes, well done everybody.

But seriously (well, you know), do you think she looked into her crystal ball before she went out shopping and thought, 'The mists still haven't cleared'? It's not the mists, you daft woman! It's your house, burning down. That's a big thing to miss for an astrology enthusiast. That's not a tall, dark stranger on the horizon – it's a bloomin' inferno!

Burnt toast starts home fire

Northampton Chronicle

Fire crews were called out to the home in Spring Gardens, Daventry at about 5.30 p.m. on Wednesday. The fire was already out by the time they arrived, but the kitchen was still smoke-logged.

■

'The fire was out'? There was no 'home fire' then, was there? Other than burning bread, that is. We've all burnt toast and I might be talking bollocks here, but I've never heard of a toast fire spreading rapidly to surrounding areas, even with a strong prevailing wind.

And 'smoke-logged'? Is that a made-up term? Have you ever heard that before?

Now THREE stories from the *same edition* of the *Wrexham Leader* ...

FLINTSHIRE LITTER BLAZE WAS ARSON, SAY FIREFIGHTERS

By Kate Forrester

Firefighters were called after rubbish was set alight on a Flintshire housing estate. North Wales Fire and Rescue Service received a call at 1.13 a.m. this morning reporting that a quantity of rubbish was on fire at South Green, Sealand. One crew from Deeside attended and used a rain jet and a hose reel to tackle the blaze. ■

They used a rain jet *and* a hose reel? Isn't that overkill?

I have tried to put myself in their position. It's a litter fire, so, 'Do we go with the hose reel or the rain jet?' 'Oh, I dunno! I can't think – it's 1.13 in the morning and we've got a quantity of burning rubbish and ... Oh, sod it! Use both, you can't be too careful with litter.'

And you know what? You can't fault the belt-and-braces approach when it comes to fire safety.

Wrexham flat blaze tackled

By Matt Sims

Firefighters were called to a flat on Crescent Road, Wrexham just before 11 p.m. last night after receiving reports of a blaze. Two appliances from Wrexham went to the scene and firefighters extinguished the flames.

■

Two stories from the same edition of the *Wrexham Leader* by two different reporters. I don't know about you, but I think Matt Sims has got a lot to learn about the journalism game. And he could do far worse than looking in his colleague Kate Forrester's direction.

Matt says firefighters were called 'just before 11 p.m.'; Kate nails the litter blaze call at 1.13 a.m. and not, as I'm suspecting Matt would have put, 'about quarter past'. Yet, Matt, even this could be excused if it wasn't for the fact that you don't tell us HOW they extinguished the flames. Was it a rain jet or a hose reel? Or both, or maybe in combination with an extinguisher?

The readers want to know – they're used to getting this vital information from Kate and you treat them with disdain. Lazy journalism or a degree of incompetence?

SMOKE ALARMS WARNING

North Wales Fire and Rescue Service is highlighting the importance of having working smoke alarms fitted after a couple escaped a fire at their Wrexham home.

At 2.30 a.m., firefighters received a report a bungalow was on fire in Bwlchgwyn.

■

I'm with them 100 per cent on this. I think you should always fit working smoke alarms. The non-working ones may be cheaper, but you will pay the price in the long run.

(A 120-point score in Scrabble.)

No reporting credit on this one, but I'm guessing Matt, purely because of the sloppy grammar.

I'll tell you what, though, there's a twisted fire starter about in Wrexham.

Nightspot damaged in blaze

Stockport Express

A Hazel Grove nightspot suffered extensive damage following a blaze on Sunday evening. Firefighters were called to the Bamboo Club at 7.19 p.m.

Four engines and twenty crew members attended. Twelve firefighters wearing breathing apparatus fought the fire with four hose reels.

A Bamboo Club? In Hazel Grove? That's an inferno waiting to happen. Bamboo and hazel *together*? A veritable tinderbox of a forest fire. How did they get planning permission for that? Some councillors got their palms greased there ...

Oh, and Matt from the *Wrexham Leader*? NB: 7.19 p.m. – not 'almost twenty past'.

Four hose reels! They don't piss about in Stockport. Well, no need to with four hose reels.

109

Two large fans were used to clear the smoke.
■

Fans? Whoa, hang about. I'm not an expert on bamboo fires, but isn't there some wise old saying about fans and flames? Something along the lines of 'Don't fan the flames'? I took this to mean that it was a bad thing to fan flames, for in doing so you supply them with more oxygen.

Now, I don't claim to be an authority (obviously), but you know when you see forest fires on TV and they have planes and helicopters dropping water? Like prolonged heavy rain? Well, this is similar, right? A bamboo forest in a Hazel Grove, so in the absence of air support, you've got to go the Wrexham route, haven't you? Minimum rain jet, plus – if possible – hose reels. If you keep fanning those flames, they will spread like, er, wildfire.

FIREMAN'S LIFT IS NOT FOR 41-STONE MAN

Daily Record

A crew of 10 firemen were called out four times in a week to lift a 41-stone man in his own home.

They travelled in two engines to Robert Marsden's council house and on one occasion were asked only to move him from one side of the bed to the other.

Ten firemen to lift a fat bloke?! Ten? ... No, really, *ten*?! Where were they lifting him up to?

Yes, but *ten*?! Unless they were moving him from the bottom bunk to the top bunk ...

And if he can't move himself around his bed, how does he get to the loo? How does he wash himself – with a rag on a stick?

Mr Marsden, 40, who is unemployed . . .

Really? You mean he doesn't work from home?

. . . and spends much of the day in bed . . .

Read 'all day' in bed, surely – he has to have firemen move him, remember?

. . . said he did not understand what the fuss was about.

Prat.

He said, 'The firemen came here and got on with their job and once they were finished, they went on to their next job. Sometimes I slide to the floor in my living room and it's hard to get back up.

'Slide'! Landslide, more like.

'My weight isn't something I like to discuss. It comes up in every conversation I have.'

■

Surprising, that. Is it usually with ten firefighters trying to roll you over? 'You're a fat sod, aren't you, Mr Marsden?'

I suggest you leave him to it. Two words: natural selection. Or leave a dead rat under his bed. He'll soon shift.

Waste not, want not

Outlook Magazine (Oxfordshire)

Would you like an extra £610 in your pocket each year?

This year has seen the nation hit by a huge increase in the cost of food and fuel, with the average cost of a basket of essentials increasing by nearly 20 per cent. A third of all food we buy goes in the bin, most of which could have been eaten.

Who wouldn't? That could buy a small terraced house in Moston or alternatively, I know ... loads of beer.

Let's work it out. £610 divided by 52 = £11.73 a week, so that's about four pints of lager ... Four?! Not even one a day, so actually, when you put it like that, it's not so great after all.

Q. So by definition, *some* of which couldn't be eaten? People are buying inedible food? Who would do that?

A. Probably the same idiots who are buying food and then going straight home to put a third of it in the bin!

The amount we throw away in a year = Wembley Stadium x 8.

Every year an average household (with children) throws out:
440,000 Ready Meals
1.3 million Unopened Yoghurt Pots
5,500 Whole Chickens

Is that a pile of food eight times bigger than Wembley Stadium? Or would it fill Wembley Stadium eight times? It's not clear. This breakdown might help ...

Every year?! Hang on a cotton-pickin' minute while I extrapolate (grammar school education). Unless my GCE Maths Grade 6 pass is on its arse, this represents the third of the food we buy that goes in the bin, right? So by my calculations, this average family (with children) actually eats in a year (i.e. doesn't throw away) the other two thirds, which works out as ...

Ready Meals 880,000
Yoghurt Pots 2.6 Million
Whole Chickens 11,000

So just how much are they eating every day? How many days in a year? Divide by 365 ...

Ready Meals 2,411
Yoghurt Pots 7,123
Whole Chickens 30

IN A DAY!

Just how big is the 'average household (with children)' down Oxfordshire way? Based on these figures, I'm guessing conservatively: Mum, Dad, Gran, Granddad and round about 300 to 400 kids, give or take.

Where did the old lady who lived in a shoe come from? You know, the one who had so many children she didn't know what to do? I bet it's the same bloody family! I bet they all live down there. All those shoe-kids have grown up long ago, had kids of their own and got their own massive council shoe houses and followed in their mother's footsteps.

Or another explanation is that there are, scattered around the nation, whole towns and villages totally inhabited by big fat Dobbers (see page 120) who are pushing the national average right up. Although I think we can discard this theory immediately, based on the fact that the only time you would ever see a Dobber with a pot of yoghurt was when they had a yeast infection – I mean, 7,123 pots *a day*? We're talking an epic fungal epidemic ... Candida-zilla.

The cost of good food thrown out per year:

TOTAL: £610.
■

£610? Where do they do their shopping? I know ALDI's cheap, but ... Do the good people of Oxfordshire go to the Gambia for the weekly big shop?

SHOP'S £4 PANTS NEARLY KILLED ME, SAYS NURSE

Evening Times, Glasgow

The Inverclyde woman bought the Meryl Skinlife body-control pants from the Primark store in Greenock, Inverclyde at the weekend.

£4 pants from Primark? No way! No underwear costs £4 in Primark, surely. I got a full dress suit there for £25. It doesn't fit me, but stuff it! £25! That's a bargain.

Having said that, they are 'Skinlife' pants and, let's face it, do sound a serious piece of kit. So perhaps it is possible that in order to justify that sort of price tag in Primark, they are actually made from real, proper skin.

117

She said that after wearing them for an hour, lumps broke out on her wrist and neck.

She said, 'It was very scary. I couldn't breathe.'

■

You need a bigger size, love. A much bigger size. The pants are squeezing all the excess fat and cellulite to the extremities of your body. This is what I believe is called 'body control' – but at its most extreme.

Get the knickers off now! Thank God the fire brigade's arrived. Tell them we've got a woman stuck in body-control pants. They're going to have to cut them off. For God's sake, everyone stand back! This could get very messy.

Dad puts brakes on speeding mobility scooters

The Northern Echo

People who drive their electric wheelchairs too fast around a town are being targeted in a safety campaign.

■

About time too. I'm sick of getting run over by Jabba the Hutt on a shopmobility as she hurtles out of Greggs on her way to Poundland for a big plastic butterfly for the side of her house.

So ... Dobbers

I've highlighted a few stories here that revolve (slowly, presumably) around fat and obese people. I have, on occasion, referred to them as 'Dobbers'. I believe that this may be a term confined to the North-West (I know, for instance, that around Nottingham a 'dobber' can be a slang term for a condom), and so I obviously need to clarify.

The first thing to say is that 'big and fat' doesn't equal 'Dobber'. Many, many people – with great personalities – are happy in their bodies and with their size: big and happy, medium and happy, small and happy. The differentiating factor is that Dobbers are big, fat, lazy, selfish slobs: quite often yobby, quite often gobby. In fact, most things that rhyme with 'dobby' – so 'slobby', there's another one.

You know the type I mean. They travel around in herds – well, they're not herds; they just look like herds, they're so big. It makes you wish we still had coyotes roaming the shopping precincts, picking off stragglers. David Attenborough doing the commentary: 'Oh no! Chantelle Demi has fallen off the pack! She's having trouble with her sausage roll. She's eaten some of the paper bag and it's stuck in her mouth ...'

Dobbers all dress the same. I'm thinking of opening a clothes shop just for them. I'm going to call it 'Dobber Clobber'. For her, the baggy T-shirts and leggings. Your female Dobber always wears leggings. Leggings are usually worn mid-calf, but on a Dobber are up round the knee as she's had to pull them up over her enormous midriff – because Dobbers have got an arse at the front as well, haven't they? I mean a proper arse with a crack in it and everything!

A particular favourite of your Dobber is the pair of lemon leggings – cheap, threadbare, bobbly leggings from Poundstretcher (and they do stretch) that she's had for months and have seen better days. And I don't know if there's a fashion magazine for Dobbers – maybe *Dobberpolitan* – but somewhere they have seen this fashion tip: 'Wearing lemon leggings? Why not set them off nicely with a pair of navy-blue knickers?' Always navy-blue knickers!

And nearly always flip-flops on their feet. Feet, by the way, which look like the feet of a griffin. Toe ring on one ('She's been tagged by the RSPB – look').

The baggy T-shirt complements the look and is quite often designer. I once saw a Dobber with the logo 'Guess' on her T-shirt, so I did. 'Thyroid problem? Big boned? Lazy slob? Give us a clue!'

She wears more gold than Mr. T ever dreamed of – the whole 'Elizabeth Duke at Argos' back catalogue, even that jointy clown pendant, the shittest piece of jewellery ever designed. Oh, and rings! As with a tree, you can tell the age of a Dobber by the number of sovereign rings she wears.

Your male Dobber, meanwhile, is often worse. More tattoos than teeth, carries a walking stick (just in case he bumps into anybody from the Social Security) and wears a Burberry baseball cap. At first glance, he appears to be dressed in a crop top – until you notice that it's actually a football shirt that can no longer accommodate his expanding gut. He will have on dirty tracksuit bottoms: le coq sportif, usually (translation: 'the sporty cock' – this from a man who's not seen his cock since 1992). On his feet: brown shoes! Brown shoes with tracksuit bottoms! When did that ever look good?

As well as dressing the same, they act the same. You can be having a quiet lunch alone in the pub, chilling out, reading the paper, when the Dobber Clan arrive. You sense that they're there almost before you hear them because you can smell pastry. And here they are: Mum, Dad and the chubby twins, Chlamydia and Fellatio.

(I once heard a Dobber mum shout for her little girl in ALDI, 'Get here now, Gethsemane Ikea!' and thought that the only two books she possessed were the Bible and an IKEA catalogue.)

In they come, invading your space – and pubs should be a sanctuary. No kids in pubs, I say: tie them up outside with a bowl of water and a tray of fish fingers.

Then the parents start shouting back and forth across the pub to each other. He yells, 'Maureen? Food?' She shouts back, 'I'll have them cheesy nachos to start, then the all-day mega breakfast, with extra chips and onion rings, and some bread and butter – two slices – and then for afters I'll have Bakewell tart and custard.'

He shouts over to her, 'Drink?' and she always pats her stomach and goes, 'Diet Coke.'

'Diet Coke'! Every time! How can that help?

Then he shouts back, 'Any more of this dieting and you'll go down the plughole,' and I can no longer restrain myself and blurt out, 'Plughole? She wouldn't go down a pissing manhole, that woman!'

BOMB 'USED AS DOORSTOP' DETONATED

Army experts have blown up what was thought to have been a WWII bomb ...

... which was found by road workers in a Ceredigion village. They carried what was believed to have been an artillery shell to an area near the local community centre.

Well, was it or wasn't it? It's a worry that bomb disposal experts aren't sure what an actual WWII bomb looks like. Haven't they got a catalogue or an *I Spy Bombs* book?

Scene: Ceredigion Village

Road Worker 1:
What do you think it is, Gareth?

Gareth:
I believe it might be an artillery shell, but we'd better ask the army experts.

Road Worker 1:
You're joking. They wouldn't know a WWII bomb if they fell over it.

Gareth:
Where shall we take it?

Road Worker 1:
Community centre?

Gareth:
Good call.

What?!

Inspector Alfor Evans from Dyfed–Powys Police said, 'There is speculation in the village that the bomb may have belonged to a local character called Dai Rogers who, it is understood, used it as a doorstop for many years.'

Speaking about the previous owner of the bomb . . .

I love 'local characters', don't you? Also, I'm thinking that Dai might have been an ex-bomb disposal expert.

Previous owner? 'For sale: bomb. As new, two previous owners, the Royal Artillery and Dai Rogers. Low mileage, genuine reason for sale.'

... author and journalist Lyn Ebenezer, who is from the village, described Mr Rogers as a 'local eccentric and inventor. He kept a monkey called Jimmy, but he was shot by the local police after he escaped and attacked a local schoolboy.

'Dai once invented a machine for generating electricity using a bicycle. But he played jokes on people, attaching wires to the doorknob of his house; when people came to call, he would jump on his bike and give them a shock.'

That's Jimmy the Monkey they shot, right?

I love Dai Rogers. What a brilliant bloke he sounds. He used a bomb as a doorstop, had a monkey called Jimmy and electrocuted visitors. There should be a film of his life.

I also think that we should examine Dai's designs for this electricity-generating bike and build thousands of them to give to old folks in winter. That would cut down the heating allowance. Get the old buggers on bikes, generating their own heat and power. They wear lots of crimplene anyway, so if we put the bikes on a nylon mat, they could top up the bike energy with static electricity, plus they'd build up a bit of a sweat after a couple of miles on programme 3 – might even be enough to take off one of their pullovers.

Dai Rogers died more than 40 years ago.
■

I hope he didn't die lonely. Yes, I know that if you went round to see him you'd get electrocuted, but I hope that didn't put his friends off too much.

'Fun' with ferrets at the YMCA

Halifax Evening Courier

Two YMCA workers used ferrets as the ball in a 'cruel' game of skittles.

The pair – a man and a woman – were captured on video flinging the pets along the shiny floor of the YMCA in Halifax.

The animals knocked down mini-skittles made from pop bottles.

Cyril Love, YMCA general secretary, confirmed the ferret-throwing game did happen.

'I saw it myself and asked for it to stop. I thought it was cruel and inappropriate.'

'It's fun to be at the YMCA' ... well, unless you're a ferret, obviously.

Why are there inverted commas around 'cruel'? Sounds full-on cruel to me.

Ferret, there's no need to feel down. Ferret, pick yourself off the ground.

Well, it keeps them off the streets.

Not so much ferret throwing as 'ferret whizzing along the floor', as the accompanying photo and caption declares.

'Inappropriate' – in what way, Cyril? As in, there is a time and a place for ferret skittles, but the YMCA is not that place?

The game was played by YMCA rollerblading supervisor Andy . . .

'Oh, I'm bored with rollerblading, let's go and chuck some defenceless animals about'

Thomas . . .

NB: Important note to the YMCA: take those rollerblades off Andy Thomas before he has a horse on them.

. . . and an unnamed female general supervisor who has since left.

I blame the parents. If they had given her a name, I doubt that she would have behaved in such an uncivilized and cruel way.

The ferrets were her pets and she told the *Courier*, 'They enjoy it because they play and bounce around. It's not dangerous.'

She was a general supervisor at the YMCA? Oh, the little furry ferrets, 'they enjoy it'! Oh, I'm sure you're right, love; having the skin burned off your paws as you whizz across the floor – bags of fun.

Andy Thomas of Pellon, Halifax, who appears in the film, defended the game, saying, 'It's not cruel. Ferrets love playing games. It's not harmful. I didn't know the film was being taken or that it was on YouTube. But it is intended to make people laugh.'

The Basic Steps for Skittles with Ferrets.

Is it cruel? See the ferret game and decide for yourself at www.halifaxcourier.co.uk.

Oh aye, it's hilarious, Andy. We all love seeing innocent animals being launched along the floor at pop bottles.

If you can believe it, the *Halifax Evening Courier* printed this on page 3 ...

... which was accompanied by four photographs of the procedure – and the opportunity for a phone vote.

They don't all work at the YMCA, do they?

IRISH JUDGE DISMISSES DRINK-DRIVE CASES DUE TO URINE STEAM INHALATION

Last month at Killorglin District Court in Kerry, two separate drink-driving cases were dismissed after the presiding judge ruled that the steam of the defendants' urine could have affected their alcohol readings taken during subsequent breath testing.

I've heard of steaming drunk, but ...

They were not the first cases that Judge O'Connor has agreed with defence submissions that inhalation of urine fumes could have skewed breath-test results and cases should be dismissed. The law requires that a person suspected of drink-driving must be observed by a garda for 20 minutes at a garda station before their breath sample is taken. During that 20-minute period, they must not consume anything by mouth.

I'm lost here. What sort of law is that? Why not get them breath-tested straight away? What's the logic behind waiting for 20 minutes, during which time the alcohol will be metabolized and the level reduced? Who first proposed this law? Mr A. Guinness?

In both cases, the solicitor, Mr O'Connell, argued that during this 20-minute period, both his clients had used a toilet to urinate.

As you do when you've been drinking all night!

Because the two men urinated with their backs to the prosecuting garda, the 20-minute observation period had been interrupted.

What?! Observing their backs doesn't count?

131

The solicitor argued that a new 20-minute observation period should have begun when his clients returned from the toilet and that the cases should be dismissed.

Judge O'Connor agreed.

He stated that the purpose of the 20-minute observation period is to ensure that nothing is taken by mouth that may affect the reading from the breath test. 'Nil by mouth is the same as nil by nose,' Judge O'Connor declared. 'When he is urinating, he is inhaling vaporized alcohol and there's always steam off it.'

Assistant Garda Commissioner Eddie Rock . . .

That, my learned friend, is – in legal terms – bollocks.

Or not! All back to Judge O'Connor's for a party.

I've heard of a 'technicality', but this is taking the piss … and then inhaling.

What a brilliant name for a top cop. Make a fantastic TV detective – 'Eddie Rock: Hard Name, Hard Man'.

... who is in charge of the Garda Traffic Corps said yesterday that the two cases which were dismissed in Killorglin served to highlight the difficulties faced by gardai in successfully prosecuting cases of alleged drink-driving. 'I don't think it is appropriate for me to say any more about it at this stage,' he said.

■

Wise move, Eddie, but if you don't mind, I will ...

First, Commissioner, do your homework and use a bit of imagination. This is preposterous. Given that, in my humble opinion, this 20-minute observation period is as dopey a law as you'll find anywhere, you have two obvious options.

1) As soon as you get the suspects to the garda station, and immediately prior to the 20-minute observation period, allow them to urinate, then start the clock. They'll have to hold it for 20 minutes. If they've not been drinking, it's not going to be a problem.

2) Watch them urinate from the front.

On another point, Eddie, regarding the inhalation of alcohol from the urine steam, how much do you reckon a person has to drink to get such a high concentration of alcohol in their urine that it affects a breath test?! Surely if the defending solicitors are arguing that the levels in urine can affect the reading, then that is in itself an admission that there is a massive amount of alcohol present in the urine. Test the urine for alcohol, Eddie.

If it helps, I might here draw on my scientific background, from whence I recall that when alcohol is metabolized in the body, less than 3 per cent of that taken in is excreted in the urine (which makes it stronger than most American beers and possibly tastier). So if 3 per cent is enough to affect a breath test, they must have had an absolute skinful.

And note to drivers in Ireland: if you're stopped by the gardai, I advise you to pee in your pants and inhale the steam; after all, it's a legitimate defence.

(That is if you're drunk, I mean – obviously. No need to do it if you've been speeding or jumped a red light.)

The day the earth shook in Lincolnshire

Skegness Standard

The *Skegness Standard* has been inundated with emails from readers telling their stories of the Lincolnshire earthquake. The earthquake struck at around 1 a.m. on Wednesday 27 February and measured 5.2 on the Richter scale.

5.2? That's quite severe, isn't it? How many casualties were there?

Emergency services report no injuries.

Ah, but there must have been extensive damage?

David Hopkins of Lincolnshire Fire said that the tremor had caused a fire when a candle fell from a TV in Skegness.

They watch the TV by candlelight in Skegness? Must have been a power cut.

Here are just some of our reader reactions …
Rachel Forman – 'I was woken last night at approximately 1 a.m. I thought my children were getting up when I felt the house shake.'

Blimey, exactly how big are your children, Rachel? The house starts shaking – and you think it's the kids getting up?

Bill Evans – 'At first I thought it was the vibration from a tractor's crawler.'

Yeah, at 1 a.m.! By the way, what exactly is a tractor's crawler?

Sylvia Colquitt – 'Ten porcelain dolls fell off the top of my wardrobe, but none of them broke.'

That's scary. She's got ten porcelain dolls on the top of the wardrobe. Fancy waking up every morning and seeing that lot staring at you.

Geoff Poulter described it as 'the worst quake he has experienced'.

Obviously an expert because he said 'quake' not 'earthquake'. But just how many earthquakes do they have down Lincolnshire way? Does the San Andreas Fault run through Skegness?

He said he heard 'dogs whimpering and birds chirping unusually'.

I say 'expert', but ... 'Dogs whimpering', fair enough, but how can you spot an 'unusual' chirp?

Mr Poulter said, 'When the tsunami happened in 2004, it was due to an earthquake underwater and it's concerning to think it could happen here.'

I take it back: he's not an expert. I doubt whether he was ever even a pert.

Rachel Forman again – 'It was like sitting on top of a washing machine.'

Was it, Rachel? And you'd know how ...?

GIRLFRIEND'S MUM HIT OVER HEAD

News & Star, Carlisle

A man appeared at Carlisle Crown Court yesterday for smashing a picture frame over a woman's head in a row over a bacon sandwich.

David Heslop, 33, of Robert Owen Avenue, pleaded guilty to common assault on Mabel Wilson, his girlfriend's mother.

Prosecutor Alan Lovett told the court Ms Wilson got home after a night out with her daughter and got into an argument with Heslop about the sandwich.

Fearing he was going to hit her daughter, Ms Wilson got in between them and tried to push him out of the way.

Beautiful.

'Mabel', that's a proper mum's name.

Fact: many food-related arguments are caused by alcohol.

It's only a sandwich!

But he retaliated by hitting her with a picture.

Now I'm not condoning his actions, far from it, but I couldn't help wondering which way he broke the picture over Mabel's head. The textbook 'Tom and Jerry' way would be in 'portrait' mode, so that her head would appear as said portrait – very funny, obviously – but I fear that because he's the sort of moron who gets violent over a bacon sandwich, he hasn't had the wit to think of this and has probably broken it 'landscape' mode over her head – not half as amusing.

Heslop, who has 52 previous convictions, including several for violence . . .

Charmer.

. . . now plans to move away from the area because that's the only way he will be able to keep out of trouble in future.

I know another way to keep him out of trouble.

I found a 'bomb' in my spuds

Liverpool Echo

Presumably when he weighed them at the self-checkout? 'There's never 5 lbs of potatoes in there! There's only three spuds and a ... is that a bomb?'

PRANK COULD HAVE LED TO ANTI-TERRORIST ALERT

Leicester Mercury

Police swooped on a student dressed as a suicide bomber who was seen running along a street in Loughborough. Officers say the man, who was carrying a toy gun, was lucky not to spark an armed response as he headed to a themed costume party at Loughborough Students' Union.

Okay, quick question: they say that he was 'dressed as a suicide bomber' – so how exactly do they dress, then? What is the well-dressed suicide bomber wearing this year? Surely if the police know, then all the millions spent on enhancing national security could be scaled down and they could just concentrate on looking out for people dressed as suicide bombers.

The student was stopped and searched on the town's Ashby Road and police confiscated the toy gun and a plastic grenade. Today, the town's police commander ...

The 'police commander' – they have a 'commander' in Loughborough, oh aye!

... issued a stern warning to students to be careful about their choice of fancy dress. Insp Mark Cuddihy said: 'I'm sure this lad thought his costume was very funny, but in the current climate you can't risk things like this. Our officers saw a young man hot-footing it up Ashby Road ...

A commander with an exceptional command of the English language. 'Our officers saw a young man hot-footing it up Ashby Road.' When have you ever heard anyone other than a policeman use the phrase 'hot-footing it'? I'll tell you when – never, that's when. I'm in my fifties and I have never used that term and I don't recall any of my friends or colleagues ever saying, 'I hot-footed it down to the market this afternoon.'

'... dressed provocatively, with a bulge in his jacket.

'Provocatively'?! How? What? Suspenders? Split-crotch tights? I know – a basque! Yes, a basque would be brilliant. Can you imagine his terror boss watching the live footage of the suicide bomber's arrest and screaming at the television: 'Imbecile! I said, "Wear a mask!" A mask!'

'He had what appeared to be a firearm. The officers stopped, searched and identified him, and established he wasn't a threat. He was extremely lucky that he was picked up by two of my bobbies.

Ouch! Have you ever been picked up by the bobbies?

'Had a member of the public called this in, there would have been no choice but to launch a full armed response. He would have ended up with a couple of laser sight dots on him and facing a large group of extremely serious armed coppers. That, I assure you, would have ruined his night.

'That, I assure you, would have ruined his night.' Textbook police-speak. You can almost see and hear him saying it, can't you?

'Armed officers have to make a snap judgement in this kind of situation. They can't tell, at forty yards, whether a gun is a toy or real. They have to decide whether to take a target out.'

Insp Cuddihy said the university had been contacted and asked to urge students to be sensible about fancy dress while in public. He said: 'We don't want to be party poopers. If students want to dress up as terrorists for fun in private ...

'... we can't tell them not to.'

One word, Commander ... binoculars.

As they do! Especially at their 'Molotov Cocktail Parties'.

Swing prank backfires

Oldham Evening Chronicle

Two girls had to call 999 after they got stuck in baby swings in Dunwood Park. Four firefighters had to turn out at around 5 p.m. yesterday to rescue the two girls aged 10 and 13 who got entangled after a dare.

Crew Commander Andrew Flynn said, 'It took two firefighters to lift each of the girls out of the swings and . . .

'. . . they certainly wouldn't have been able to get out on their own.

Listen to this gem.

No shit, Crew Commander! We know that they couldn't get out on their own. That's why they dialled 999, remember? And by the way, how big were these ten- and thirteen-year-old girls that it took two firefighters per girl? That's what I call puppy fat.

He's not finished yet.

'It was a very foolish thing to do and if they had thought before they got into the swings, they would have known they couldn't get out again.'
■

No wonder he's made it to Crew Commander.

Same story, but let us compare and contrast the styles – we'll start with the *Mirror* …

MY HENS ARE BEING KILLED BY BALLOONS

Daily Mirror

A farmer's hens are dying because hot-air balloons are causing their eggs to burst open inside them.

Abbi Vincent-Lloyd claims the stress of seeing the floating giants makes her birds run in fear and bump into obstacles and each other.

Abbi, 32, lost 30 hens when balloons …

… and low-flying RAF jets …

Killer balloons? We could be in Narnia.

Are you sure it's not a hot-air microwave oven? My one makes eggs burst.

A floating giant would probably make me run and bump into things.

Balloons?! They're frightened of balloons? Chickens.

Oh, jets? I sort of get that – they scramble the jets; they scrambled some eggs.

... were operating over her land at Caplor Farm in the Wyre Valley, Herefordshire. She said, 'I told the vet about the balloons and jets and he said straight away that was the cause. The hens go crazy when they are about.

'They bump into things and their eggs explode. It's a horrible way to go.'

Their eggs then crack open causing internal infections.

■

They run around like headless chi ... er.

You're not kidding there. It's like they're carrying a ticking time bomb inside them. Well, chicken tikka time bomb.

Be funny, though, don't you think? I mean, don't get me wrong, I love chickens and I'm heavily into animal welfare, but a chicken running into a tree and there's a sudden 'boom' and ... 'Broadsword calling Danny Boy – one of our hens is missing.'

Shell shock.

Let's turn to the BBC ...

Balloons 'scared hens to death'

Free-range chickens at a farm in Herefordshire were 'scared to death' ...

... by the noise of hot-air balloons flying overhead, their owner has claimed. The 300 hens at Caplor Farm in Fownhope were sent 'wild' ...

... by the noise of the hot-air balloons' gas burners.

Abbi Vincent-Lloyd said 10 per cent of the hens had died from panic-related injuries since the balloons began flying in July.

The use of inverted commas here suggests the BBC is not *quite* so convinced by the 'killer balloons' theory ...

See what I mean?

Weren't they pretty much 'wild' already? Or am I missing the intention behind 'free range'?

Slap an ASBO on those balloons. That's what they did to my neighbour when he was playing Wimbledon videos at four in the morning – and that racket really would scare you to death.

I have a few ex-battery chickens and they *are* prone to panicking at the slightest thing. They need a Corporal Jones in amongst them shouting, 'Don't panic! Don't panic!' One of my chickens, Lesley (I give them names), panicked because my turkey Bertie jumped on her for a laugh and she broke her leg. I took her to the vet's and I thought he'd say, 'Brick it,' which I believe is a technical expression, but he didn't, he put a little plaster cast on her leg and she's back in the garden now and what's nice is that all the other chickens have signed it – 'Keep your pecker up,' that sort of thing.

You can't steer a hot-air balloon: fact.

I'm not so sure. I suspect that the balloon company fly over Caplor Farm on purpose – I think that watching chickens go crazy is in fact their in-flight entertainment! I bet this particular balloon excursion is called 'Chicken Impossible'.

I rest my case. I think it's all part of a package deal – bringing a whole new meaning to those murder-mystery weekends.

Miss Vincent-Lloyd added: 'The hens don't notice the balloons going over until they turn on the gas.

Silent But Deadly.

'It throws them into chaos ...

I'm not surprised, are you? Two words, Miss Vincent-Lloyd: *Chicken Little*. Did they not teach you Buddhist Indian folklore at chicken-farming school?

'... they bash into things and each other in their rush to get inside ...

Sounds like the January sales. Except the '10 per cent off' means something completely different here.

'... which is when their eggs crack.'
■

Chickens are prone to cracking up. After all, we're talking about an animal here that once thought the sky was falling down because an acorn fell on its head.

I can see Miss Vincent-Lloyd staring at the page blankly, mouth agape with a 'What the hell are you talking about?' expression. So for her information, there are many versions of the *Chicken Little* story. This is one.

> Once upon a time, as a chicken was eating her lunch one day, an acorn fell on her head. She believed the sky was falling down and decided to tell the King.

Now, you might think that because she thought the sky was falling down, chickens are a bit dim – but I would say in their defence that they are not so dim as not to know that if the sky is falling down, you go straight to the top.

On her journey to the palace, Chicken Little encountered many other creatures, who joined her in her quest. (In most versions of this tale, the animals all have rhyming names, such as Henny Penny, Cocky Lockey and Goosey Loosey.)

Finally, the group came across Foxy Loxy, a fox ...

Never!

... who offered the chicken and her chums his charming assistance ...

Watch out! Chickens don't have many faults in my eyes, but they can certainly be too trusting.

After this point, there exist a variety of conclusions to the fable ...

In the most familiar one, Foxy Loxy eats the chicken's friends, but the last one standing – usually Cocky Lockey – survives long enough to forewarn the chicken, and she manages to escape.

'Survives long enough'? That doesn't sound so good. Still, Chicken Little has escaped – give the cock a medal.

Some endings depict Foxy eating them *all*.

What sort of a story is that for children to read?!

In other versions, the main characters are rescued by a squirrel or an owl, and actually get the chance to speak to the King himself.

A squirrel *or* an owl? I know that they've both got big eyes and live in trees, but surely even a chicken could tell the difference?

In yet another variation, the chums are sometimes saved by the
King's hunting dogs.

I'm wondering if that should read 'savaged' not 'saved'. Only I had an
Alsatian once who ripped two chickens to bits for a laugh.

And one version ends with the sky falling ... and killing
Foxy Loxy.

I'm all for that. That's my favourite – the sky falls on the fox. Just the
fox. Missed everybody else so ... probably not the sky, then. Probably
a meteorite or something.

Depending on the conclusion, the moral changes.

Get out of here! Really? But they're so similar (not).

In the 'happily ever after' version, the moral is not to be a
'chicken', but to have courage. In other versions, the moral is
widely considered to suggest 'do not believe everything you
are told'.

Or how's this for a clearer moral? If you're stupid, you might die.

LPG car explodes as driver lights a cigarette

Daily Telegraph

Peter Tidbury had just filled up his Peugeot 607 with 40 litres of gas at a service station and was driving at around 30 mph. He could smell gas in the car and passed it off as remnants from the petrol station.

Mr Tidbury decided to smoke a cigarette.

The second he ignited the lighter its flame sparked a fireball.

As I said: if you're stupid, you might die.

LPG ... That's Liquefied Petroleum *Gas*, isn't it?

Picture the scene, then: you've just put 40 litres of GAS in your tank and you can smell GAS in the car – what would your next step be?

Beautiful. This is natural selection in action.

LPG – it does exactly what it says on the pump.

The windows were blown out and the bonnet and the boot were thrown open by the force of the blast. His clothes melted on him ...

Mr Tidbury has ruled out buying another LPG car and intends to quit smoking.

Ah, but you've got to laugh, haven't you? No, really, I pissed myself. It's a scene straight from a 'Laurel and Hardy' film – Olly's sat there with a shredded exploded cigar in his mouth, his face black with smoke, his bowler hat and clothes smouldering ...

It is somewhat surprising that someone who was environmentally aware enough to buy an LPG car was also a smoker.

Now TWO stories from the *same edition* of the *Oldham Advertiser* ...

FARMERS FEAR RETURN OF 'SADDLEWORTH SAVAGE'

The mutilated remains of a dead lamb have again triggered fears that a mysterious cat may be stalking the moors above Saddleworth villages. The carcass of the lamb was found near a wall in a field owned by one of the area's biggest sheep farmers.

The father of three said, 'The lamb had blood lacerations to its neck. It almost looked as though it had been butchered by a professional.

Go on. How big is he, this farmer?

So, rather than looking for a mysterious cat, we should be looking for a rogue butcher?

'I just hope we don't have a puma or other such animal on the loose here.

Me too – especially one of those 'other such' animals. They are vicious.

'I am concerned and wonder if anyone else has seen any kind of wild animal on my land or nearby.'

Yeah, as if you'd seen it, but then it had slipped your mind. That could happen.

'Now you come to mention it, I did see something, but I thought it was simply a big mysterious cat, but it could have been a puma or a panther just acting a bit daft, like.'

In December 2003, several people claimed to have seen a black panther near Dovestones reservoir. Then three years later, in Uppermill, patrons of the Church Inn and walkers saw a large black cat described by landlord Michael Taylor and his grandson Ayrton ...

Ayrton?!

... as 'four times the size of a normal cat, with a snarl on its face, pointed elfin ears and moving very fast'.

We don't like strangers round here.

POOCH BACK WITH THE 'PACE' AFTER £8,500 OPERATION

Floyd the Saddleworth boxer dog is fighting fit …

… after having a pacemaker fitted to his heart in a rare operation. Floyd remains on medication.

Floyd's recovery has also been aided by 40-minute walks on fields around Saddleworth.

■

Are you thinking what I'm thinking?

So we have a boxer dog on medication …

On a special diet of lamb, is he?

Crisps assault

Northants Evening Telegraph

A man had a packet of crisps tipped over him out of a car window.

Just how tall was this man? If they could tip crisps over him from a car window, he either has to be tiny or crawling home or having a lie-down, maybe?

Police are treating the incident between 5.10 and 5.15 p.m. ...

About quarter past five, then?

... on Saturday as assault.
■

Assault with 'a-salted' crisp, that is.

HE TOOK MY KIDNEY, THEN BROKE MY HEART

Metro

This story is just as it sounds: a wife donates a kidney to her husband, who – pretty much as soon as the stitches are out – runs off with another woman; which is odd because it's usually the organ they reject, isn't it? Not the actual donor …

Here's a suggestion for the judge, though. Why don't you award the kidney back to her in the divorce settlement? Or half at least. Half would be fair.

Jealous wife set husband's genitals on fire

A wife who set her husband's genitals on fire because she suspected him of an affair has been charged with his murder.

Rajini Narayan, 44, told neighbours she was a 'jealous wife' but she had not meant to kill him when she doused the sleeping man's genitals with an alcohol-based solvent and then set him on fire.

The husband jumped out of bed and knocked over the bottle of alcohol, causing the fire to spread.

Tragic story, of course, and I've tried to put myself in the husband's place. Tried to imagine sleeping soundly one minute, then awakening – in terror – with your private parts ablaze. Can you think of a worse way to be woken up?

I know, I've sprung the question on you suddenly and you may need time to think about it – whereas I've had that benefit and have come up with three other terrifying scenarios, which I hereby submit for your consideration. Being woken by ...

1) The soil hitting your coffin lid.
2) Somebody slapping your face and screaming, 'Wake up, infidel dog!'
3) That weird 'thup thup thup' sound as your front wheels cross onto the hard shoulder of the motorway.

Speaking of which, I read somewhere recently that 50 per cent of motorists have admitted to falling asleep while driving on the motorway and drifting onto the hard shoulder. Of that 50 per cent, I reckon the last words most of them remember before dozing off were: 'And now, the new single from Ronan Keating ...'

Two women arrested at Leeds 'brothel'

Yorkshire Evening Post

Police have shut down a suspected brothel and arrested two women accused of working there.

Following complaints from neighbours, officers raided the property in Bayswater Row, Harehills, on Wednesday. No one was in the house at the time ...

The smallest little whorehouse in Yorkshire.

Only two women, eh? Is that a quorum?

Definition: 'quorum' – the minimum number of members of an organization required to conduct business.

Ho, ho! I think I've found a loophole here and I'm talking a legal loophole, not *loop-hole*, the type of repetitive strain injury to which working girls are susceptible.

D'oh! How dim are the police? It's half-day closing on Wednesday (shops, legs, etc.). The girls need time off to recharge their batteries.

... but during a search, police found items related to the sex industry.

While police were securing the building ...

... two women, aged 43 and 51, arrived at the house ...

... and were arrested on suspicion of using the address as a brothel.

Inspector Nik Adams, who leads the Gipton and Harehills Neighbourhood Policing Team, said: 'This should serve as a demonstration that we will tackle all forms of vice ...

' ... and I would encourage local residents to report any suspicious activity to their local neighbourhood policing team.' Anyone wishing to pass information to police can call this number.
■

See – items with batteries.

'Securing the building'? Do they mean locking up? It's a suspected brothel, not a terrorist cell.

Aged 43 and 51? Imagine that! No, second thoughts, don't! I bet they walk like John Wayne after five days in the saddle.

Would you like to rephrase that, Inspector?

Yeah, right, that's going to happen.

Strangely, this was the third similar story to surface during my tour. One was reported on the local lunchtime news, when a young reporter was despatched to present a live report from outside the house of ill repute, which, as it happened, was situated in a quiet residential area. He started off with the usual voiceover: 'At first glance, this looks like an innocent-looking house in an innocent street.'

I'm not sure how houses look innocent, are you? What does a guilty house look like; has it got the blinds half down?

Then he carries on with the report that this so-called 'massage parlour' has been found to be operating as a brothel. (Get away! Really? Not just massage, then?) He informs viewers that the police have applied to the courts to have it closed down, but until such time as the case can be heard, the parlour is still open for business (great PR coup for the brothel), much to the dismay and disgust of some local residents.

Just then, one of the working girls appears at the front door and proceeds to light up a fag. Our young reporter makes an instinctive, executive decision. 'I see one of the girls has popped out for a moment. Let's see if she'll have a quick word with me.'

You can almost see and feel the panic from behind the camera; you can imagine the commotion back in the studio – it's lunchtime news, after all, what is he thinking?

The reporter approaches the young lady – 'Erogenique', as it turns out – and suggests to her that this is an unusual location for such an establishment, here in the quiet residential neighbourhood. She just shrugs and says that, as it happens, they're always very busy.

'Really?' he says. 'How busy?'

So she says, 'Well, let's just put it this way, I've been up and down those stairs twenty-eight times today.'

He pauses for thought and then comes out with, 'Oh, your poor ... feet.' Feet?!

And that's not the end of it as we go back to the studio, where the flustered anchorman almost tops this when he reads out a statement issued by the local police, who appeal to the residents to have patience until after the court hearing and, I quote, 'not to take matters into their own hands'.

GREAT TITS COPE WELL WITH WARMING

© bbc.co.uk/news

One of Britain's birds appears to be coping well as climate change alters the availability of key food.

■

No, really.

One? There's just one bird coping well? Not much to shout about, is it? I mean, well done and all that, but shouldn't we be concentrating on finding ways to persuade it to show all its mates how it's done? Selfish tit.

However, the award for Best Headline in a Local Newspaper goes to ...

INN SPECTRE CALLS AS SPIRITS IN BAR BLAMED FOR MISCHIEF

The Northern Echo

Gin, whisky and rum are top-shelf staples of pubs. But spirits of another kind are also abundant in The Foresters Arms near Darlington, according to the pub's landlady, who says she was mysteriously locked in the beer cellar overnight. 37-year-old Kate Umpleby . . .

A cut above your normal headline. This play on words not only references the J. B. Priestley classic, it also incorporates the inventive use of 'spectre' and 'spirits', evoking ghostly goings-on. Take a bow, Jim Entwistle at *The Northern Echo*.

Good name. (There's a photo and she is a looker, by the way.)

... who has been running the pub for only two weeks, had checked that the pub was empty. Kate spent nine hours in the chilly cellar of the pub in Coatham Mundeville when the door to the room slammed and locked behind her. The pub is being renovated and to stop punters falling downstairs, workmen have fitted a bolt to the beer cellar door.

When Miss Umpleby's boyfriend returned on Monday morning ...

... he found the bolt locked, but no sign of intruders.

■

Genuinely scary. I can understand the door slamming, but I have no idea how the bolt got fastened.

Although! Where's he been, then?

He did it, didn't he? Locked her in there overnight for a laugh, or any number of other reasons, in my opinion.

Finally, the award for Best Headline in a National Newspaper goes to ...

Seedy Gonzales jailed in lesbo sperm swindle

The Sun

John Gonzales, 45, hit the headlines ...

... when he started an Internet firm charging £2,000 a time to women who wanted a tot.

'Lesbo sperm swindle' ... what a headline! It's got everything. It's funny, it's factual and it's offensive.

Oh, I see! Gonzales! 'Seedy' Gonzales – genius. We can modify the original song now ... 'Hey Rosita, come quick! Down at the sperm bank they're giving green stamps away with spermatozoa!'

Full marks for the ambiguity of 'women who wanted a tot'. I'd like to think they meant both definitions – as in 'baby' tot and also 'a small measure' tot ... although I'm not sure how much a tot of sperm is as they usually measure it in teaspoons, don't they?

Gonzales, who called himself the Stelios of Sperm . . .

. . . and lived the high life on the Costa del Sol in Spain, owed £21,000 to the courier firm that delivered the samples.

It is still unclear where Gonzales obtained the sperm. Health experts warned that buying sperm over the Internet was dangerous. It could be riddled with disease or even come from animals.

■

So EasyJiz, then?

That would be 'Come Quickly Transport'.

I don't know about you, but I find that very difficult to swallow. (Sorry, I needed an 'out'.)

BOG-SNORKELLER 'DISGUSTED' BY COMEDY SKETCH

A company behind a controversial show airing on RTÉ has rejected a claim from Ireland's champion bog-snorkeller that her good name has been tarnished in a mud-wrestling comedy sketch.

Julia Galvin (38) from Listowel, Co Kerry . . .

. . . has complained she was left 'disgusted, appalled and shocked' . . .

Not 'tarnished', surely? Good name has been 'dragged through the mud' is better.

Bit old for a bog-snorkelling champion?

Appalled and shocked? Same thing, really?

Wife-carrying! That sounds like a great sport. In fact, it would be brilliant if there was a whole athletic event devoted to wife-related sports: wife-carrying, wife-tossing, wife-rolling-down-a-hill, heavyweight wife-lifting, hop, skip and a jump (we've all been that excited), etc. Oh, I do hope that somewhere there's a wife-carrying relay race, in which wives are passed from one carrier to the next. That'd be brilliant. I wonder what the rules to wife-carrying are? Do you have to carry your own wife?

On a serious note, I would like to bring something to the judges' attention. *Ms* Galvin is not eligible for wife-carrying! Ms Galvin isn't married and should be barred.

... had turned down an invitation to appear as a mud wrestler on the television show. 'I decided it wouldn't be for me,' she said. However, she said the comedy show had then went on to use a lookalike ...

'Had then went on'! She's a substitute teacher, this woman.

... and introduced her as Ireland's bog-snorkelling champion, under a different name. The sketch featured two women kissing after wrestling in the mud.

What channel was this on again? Can I get it on iPlayer? Is a repeat scheduled?

'I find it baffling why they had to use someone who looked the image of me,' she said, adding that she had contacted solicitors to deal with the matter. 'I refused to do mud wrestling ... and the next thing, there are women kissing.' Ms Galvin said she was left shocked by it. 'I refused to do mud wrestling ... and the next thing, there are women kissing,' she said.

Is there an echo in here?

'It's embarrassing, it has made me a source of ridicule,' she added.

No, not a 'source' of ridicule, a 'subject' of ridicule. It is absolutely no surprise to me that she's only a substitute teacher. Stick to the bog-snorkelling, love.

'I'm a bubbly, happy kind of person and this has left me subdued.'

Look, it was a comedy show and they didn't say it was you; and after all, the bottom line is, how many people in the country could actually name or identify or even, let's face it, care a flying toss who the bog-snorkelling champion of Ireland is?

'Sportswoman'?! You having a laugh?

In March, the sportswoman ...

... is due to travel to a bog-snorkelling competition in Julia Creek, Queensland, Australia, where she will represent Ireland.

■

Julia Creek? That's a place not a person, right? No relation to Jonathan? Because I'm telling you now, 'Bog-snorkelling in Julia Creek' sounds like a DVD you can buy off Pineapple Pete's stall on Chorley Market.

Should Lunt alter village name to stop sign vandals?

Liverpool Daily Post

Mmm, tricky one, this.

The name of a historic Merseyside village was under threat last night after a prospective Conservative councillor launched a campaign that could see it changed.

Typical dumb Tory: aspires to be councillor and his first campaign is to change the name of this historic (that's historic) village. That'll go down well with the locals, I expect. How dim do you have to be?

Martyn Ball, who is standing for election in Sefton's Park ward, says Lunt should be changed to Launt.

And Martyn should be spelt with an 'i' not a 'y'.

This would stop vandals tampering with the lettering on signs in the village and embarrassing the locals, he says.

Grow up, Ball. You've seen it once, you've seen it a hundred times and although I've never been to Lunt, I would bet that most of the locals in this Merseyside village aren't at all embarrassed.

Dr Ball ...

Ah, 'Dr' is it now?

... a retired police officer ...

It's becoming clearer...

... with 23 years' experience ...

Twenty-three years' experience. So retired at what, about forty years old? Too much time on his hands.

... said, 'The problem over the years is the sign past the village gets defaced by mindless vandals into an old Anglo-Saxon word.'

I beg to differ. If they deface the sign into an old Anglo-Saxon word, I would suggest that this is far from 'mindless' – on the contrary, very inventive and knowledgeable. I don't know anyone who is conversant with Anglo-Saxon vocabulary.

Dr Ball is canvassing opinion in the village ahead of May elections. He says he will only take the proposal to Sefton council if he has villagers' backing.

Well, I think he's an idiot. But what do the villagers think?

Stewart Dobson, an 84-year-old Sefton Parish councillor, described the proposal as 'ridiculous'. 'I've been on the Parish Council for 30 years. All the older people who've lived here for donkeys ...

His words, not mine. Each to their own – if people live for donkeys, who are we to criticize?

'... none of them want to change. This village is very, very old and people don't want the name changed. I don't know the logic behind it ...

Unfamiliar with Anglo-Saxon.

... and all for one little sign. It's ridiculous.'

Yes, it is. Of course it is. All right-minded people would think that, apart from Dr Martyn Ball, who is the mindless vandal in all this.

Mr Dobson said that tape is stuck on the 'L' of the sign to change its spelling ...

Yeah, we sort of got that, Mr Dobson.

... but the tape falls off in the rain.

So, given the prevailing weather on Merseyside, it's hardly ever on for very long, is it?

According to local website www.lunt-village.co.uk, the village was first referred to in records in 1251 in the 'Chartulary of Cockersand Abbey'.

Ohmigod! 'Cockersand'? Don't tell Dr Ball, whatever you do. He'll want to change that as well. To 'Corkersand' or something equally absurd.

The name is derived from the Norse word 'lundr' ...

They weren't big on vowels, your Norse; they'd have been rubbish on *Countdown*.

... or the Swedish word 'lunder' ...

They'd be all right.

... which both mean 'copse' or 'grove'.

Make your mind up.

David Roughley, whose family has farmed in the village since 1851, said, 'At the end of the day, we live in Lunt.'

And at the beginning and in the middle.

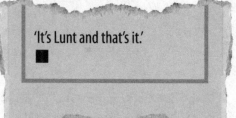

'It's Lunt and that's it.'

Absolutely. And just as a footnote to the feeble-minded Dr Ball: you think that changing Lunt to Launt will solve the problem?! Even the most mindless of vandals could easily change that. You've still left the 'unt' together, you idiot, so that all they have to do is tape out the 'L' and change the 'a' to a 'C'. Thing is, he can't see that – he has to be the stupidest man in the village.

NB: Memo to Lunt council. For a laugh, may I strongly suggest that you twin Lunt with the picturesque Swiss village of Lagina, just to see Ball's face when the twinning sign goes up: 'LUNT twinned with LAGINA.' Pass me the tape.

JURORS VIEW VIDEOTAPED INTERVIEW OF PRITCHARD

The Hutchinson News

Aron Pritchard told a detective that he put his girlfriend's children in a clothes dryer because he wanted to show them they could have a good time without much money.

That's 'without *much* money', so I'm thinking he actually did charge them a nominal amount. I wonder what else he had lined up for them? Towing them behind his car on a bin lid? Surfing on an ironing board?

Pritchard told juvenile detective Ernie Underwood …

The last thing you need is a 'juvenile' detective …

Scene: Police Interview Room

Ernie Underwood:
(Produces notebook)
Name?

Pritchard:
Pritchard.

Ernie Underwood:
(Giggles)
Pilchard? You're a pilchard. Ha, ha, ha …
(Prods Pritchard's chest with his pencil)
What's that?

(Pritchard looks down, and Ernie flicks his pencil up,
smacking Pritchard's nose.)

Ernie Underwood:
Ha, ha, ha, ha … Gotcha! Na, na, na, na, na.

Pritchard:
What the f – ?

Ernie Underwood:
First name?

Pritchard:
Aron.

Ernie Underwood:
(Giggles even more as he writes in his notebook)
Hairy Pilchard – that's you, that is.
(Laughs and sings)
Hairy Pilchard, Hairy-Hairy Pilchard!

... that he had been playing with the then 2-year-old girl and 3-year-old boy on 28 November by rolling them round in a large cardboard barrel that served as a toy box.

Kids love playing with the box more than the toy that comes in it, don't they?

The activity began to aggravate an old shoulder injury ...

Presumably sustained when he was hang-gliding off the roof with a bed sheet ...

... and Pritchard said that he could no longer push the children.

How big were these kids? They're only two and three years old!

He said he remembered playing in an old dryer as a child ...

Well, you'd not forget that, would you?

... and wanted to show the children a good time.

I wonder if he put 'Bounce' in to soften the ride?

'That's what I wanted to show my kids, that you don't need to have money to have a good time. All you have to have is an imagination.'

Not much imagination in my book. Let's face it, a much better ride would have been in the washing machine on fast spin – that's a proper ride, that is. You ask my son Stephen.

Pritchard said that the dryer door was open and he was kneeling with his hand on the kill switch ...

The *what*?!

... while the children took turns riding in the machine.

Get 'em in together.

However, after about an hour of playing, the dryer heated up and gave the boy second-degree burns.

1) It took an hour to heat up? That is one rubbish clothes dryer – we need to know the make. Probably a cheap import called something like 'Aisungosonic Thermohot'.

2) The kid should count himself lucky (can you count when you're three?) he only got second-degree burns. At least he's got a clothes dryer – we had a mangle when I was growing up. If Aron Pritchard had been around then, injuries would've been far more severe.

'I didn't mean for my boy to get hurt,' Pritchard told the detective.

■

And you know what? Even though he had his finger on the 'kill switch' (!), I believe him. I think he was, in a rather eccentric – all right, stupid – way, trying to teach the children a valid lesson: how to make your own fun. I'm of the strong opinion that we should all make our own fun on a regular basis – and here are a few suggestions of things you could try:

1) Next time Debenhams or TK Maxx have got a big sale on and they cram so many clothes onto a rail that you can hardly move them, go and hide behind the rail. Crouch down out of sight and when a woman starts looking through, say in a loud, plaintive voice, 'Pick me … Pick me …' That really freaks them out.

2) When you see a church wedding taking place, sneak in and sit at the back. When it comes to the bit where the vicar/priest says, 'If anyone here knows of any reason why these two people should not be joined together in holy matrimony …' (followed by that nervous silence), put your hand up and shout, 'Yes, here!' Everyone will turn and stare at you aghast, so leave it for a minute and then put your hand down and mutter, 'No, it's all right, forget it. Doesn't matter. It was only once … and I think he was discovering his sexuality.' Then stroll out.

3) Next time a group of you goes out for a meal, one of you should order the asparagus starter. Then, when the waitress brings the starters and says, in waitress-speak, 'Who's asparagus?' you say, 'I'm asparagus' – then quickly, as she makes her way over to you (and before she can set the plate down), another person stands up and says, 'No, I'm asparagus.' Then another, then another …

4) In Debenhams again, or your local clothes store, go into the changing rooms and draw the curtains across or close the door, then wait for an assistant to pass by. Position your head about halfway down and then peep out and say, 'Excuse me, can you get me some toilet paper, please? There's none in this one.'

5) On your next flight, after the drinks and food have been served and there's a bit of a lull in proceedings, press the 'Call' button. When the stewardess leans over and quietly asks you what you want, shout out really loud: 'NO, I CAN'T FLY A PLANE! WHAT MAKES YOU THINK I CAN FLY A PLANE?!'

Jumping cow crash farmers cleared

Two farming brothers have been cleared of blame over a road accident caused by a cow which became a 'wild animal' when separated from its calf.

The cow jumped a six-bar gate and died when it was hit by a car as it stood in the road.

The Court of Appeal ruled that the farmers could not have known about the cow's 'exceptional jumping ability'.

The judges found that although recently weaned cows have a desire to return to their calves, the cause of the accident was this cow's 'exceptional jumping ability', which was not known to the farmers.

■

'Became' a wild animal?

How can you not avoid a big cow stood in the road?

Cows can jump as high as they want to, it's just that generally they don't feel like it.

Complete this well-known verse, phrase or saying: 'Hey diddle diddle, the cat and the fiddle, the cow jumped over ...' They knew all right.

185

TIGER VICTIM COMFORTABLE

Derry Journal

The condition of the Claudy teenager who was mauled in the arm by a tiger at Dublin Zoo last week . . .

. . . was yesterday described as 'comfortable'.

It had been thought that 19-year-old Roisin Brolly from the Foreglen Road would be moved to Altnagelvin Hospital yesterday morning to receive medical treatment closer to her family home.

'CLAUDY GIRL CLAWED' would have been a better headline. And thinking about it, it was fated to happen to someone from Claudy at some date, wasn't it?

'Comfortable'?! She got mauled by a tiger! She can't be comfortable; unless they mean she's well off financially, or they've got her bandaged up in traction and the doctors and nurses are sitting on her, having a cup of tea and saying, 'She's quite comfortable, isn't she?'

Great name, 'Brolly', by the way. Not related to any of the Golfin' Brollys, is she?

However the James Connolly Memorial Hospital in Dublin last night said that Ms Brolly would remain there for the time being.

They also said that the teenager was in a 'comfortable condition'. The former Thornhill student sustained serious injuries to her arm when she reportedly climbed into the animals' enclosure during a visit on Wednesday. She was rushed to James Connolly Memorial Hospital where she underwent emergency surgery to save her arm. It is understood Ms Brolly climbed a solid six-foot timber fence and then a four-foot wall into the tigers' enclosure.

A talking hospital!

A solid six-foot fence? What's the point of that in a zoo? How can you see the animals? You'd have to climb up it to peep over the top at the big cats, wouldn't you?

And let me get this straight: there is only a six-foot fence and a four-foot wall keeping the tigers in? A frog could jump over that, never mind one of nature's most agile killing machines. That can't be safe, surely. Get Claims Direct on the phone – Zoological Division.

At the time of the attack, two of the rare big cats were resting in the enclosure and one lunged at her, grabbing her arm, and tried to pull her through.

'Pull her through' where, exactly? The keyhole? The hedge backwards?

Ms Brolly's companion raised the alarm ...

She was with someone?! She was with someone who didn't try to stop her climbing over the fence into the tigers' den?! Call yourself a friend? Well, no, obviously, that's why you are now only a 'companion'.

... and the injured woman was taken to hospital for treatment.

Leo Oosterweghel, director of Dublin Zoo ...

That would be Leo 'The Lion' Oosterweghel?

... said that Ms Brolly's injuries were 'significant'.

Usually the case with a tiger attack, I'm guessing. You wouldn't get a 'trivial' mauling, would you?

He added, 'The tiger really ripped into her arm and must have pulled her arm through when she stuck it in.'

I say again, 'pulled her arm through' and 'stuck it in' where? We've established that she was in the enclosure and that's mad enough; now she's sticking her arm somewhere she shouldn't? Crazy woman.

Mr Oosterweghel said that the tigers, which can grow up to 3.5 metres in length ...

I think we know how big tigers are, Leo. I don't think length is an important factor here. I doubt if Ms Brolly landed in the enclosure and went, 'Bloody hell, they're a lot bigger than I thought.' I've only ever seen them on the television and they were only three or four inches tops there.

... reacted as they would in the wild and would not be put down.

It's a well-known fact that tigers will only attack humans when they feel like it.

The zoo is reviewing its security, but the incident is not likely to result in more fencing around the enclosure.

■

You know what? There's something not right about this story. I don't think she was actually inside the enclosure. Surely even in Dublin they don't think that a six-foot fence and a four-foot wall is sufficient caging for tigers?

I think from the way the report highlights the fact that Ms Brolly 'stuck her arm in' and was pulled through something or other there was probably a proper metal enclosure on the other side of the fence and wall. I think she stuck her arm through, possibly trying to feed the tigers a sandwich or something.

Scene: Outside the Tiger Enclosure, Dublin Zoo

Ms Brolly:
(Shouts down from top of solid six-foot fence)
Do you want this last chicken sandwich?

Companion:
No, why?

Ms Brolly:
I'm going to give it to the tigers. They look hungry.

Companion:
The tigers look hungry?!

Ms Brolly:
Yes.
(Jumps over fence, vaults over ineffective four-foot wall and sticks her arm through enclosure fence. Offers sandwich to tigers.)
Come on then … Ch ch ch ch … Who's a good boy, then?

(Tiger approaches and chomps her arm – either because tigers have very poor spatial awareness, or because they prefer a nice juicy arm to a chicken buttie.)

I'd love to think that she now did that thing that we do when we stupidly hurt ourselves in public, but pretend we haven't done so in order to save embarrassment. You know when you walk into a lamp post because you're not looking properly, and you fracture your skull and there's blood coming out of your eyes, but all that you're bothered about is that someone might have seen you and you can't let them know it hurt like hell.

So I'd love to think that she stood there with her ragged stump of an arm and her companion said, 'God! Are you all right?' and she replied, 'Who, me? Yeah. I'm always doing this! What am I like?'

Homeless woman banned from driving

Lancaster Guardian

Beverley Ann Charnock, 46, of Melling, Carnforth pleaded guilty at South Lakeland Magistrates Court to drink-driving after she was stopped by police in Kirkby Lonsdale in the early hours of January 16.

Where was she off to then?

Scene: Roadside

Police Officer:
Okay, Lewis flaming Hamilton, where are you off to in such an almighty hurry at this time of night?

Homeless Woman:
Well, er ... nowhere, really.

The court heard how two police officers, who were on duty in the town, saw Charnock crash her car into a wall while trying to execute a three-point turn near the public toilets at Devils Bridge.

You'd have to be well pissed to try to do a three-point turn at a place called Devils Bridge! That's a scary place at the best of times. How scary? I'll tell you. So scary that they have had to put some public toilets there.

ONE MAN WENT TO MOW ... NAKED!

The Press, York (January)

A man has appeared in court charged with indecent exposure after his neighbours spotted him gardening in the nude.

Yan Price, 30, is said to have mowed the lawn in his back garden while naked, but was spotted by his neighbours, two of them serving North Yorkshire police officers.

Howard Shaw, prosecuting, told York Crown Court ...

... that a female neighbour who cannot be named for legal reasons ...

Doing a bit of pricking out, presumably.

Nabbed by the fuzz.

It's gone to Crown Court! How pathetic is that?

What legal reasons? We know she lives next door, on the other side to the police officers – narrows it down a bit.

... was in bed one Sunday morning when she heard Price start up his mower. The young mother peered through her bedroom window to see Price in his garden tending to the lawn wearing a pair of shorts. Mr Shaw said the neighbour again looked out of the window, but this time saw something she did not expect.

'She could see the defendant out in the garden and he wasn't wearing a stitch of clothing. He was completely naked using the lawnmower,' he told the jury.

Price is also charged with breaching an ASBO which banned him from speaking to his neighbours, North Yorkshire police officers Tracy and Paul Rogers.

I'm not so sure, are you?

It's January, it's freezing, he's naked ... I'm surprised she could see anything to offend her.

How did he get the ASBO, I wonder? Can't be just for gardening in the nude in Scarborough. I know it's Yorkshire and they're made of strong stock, but it's freezing at the best of times up there, and as I said before, this is January and he's out there stark naked – he deserves a medal, not an ASBO.

He (Mr Shaw) said the group had felt intimidated on many occasions after complaining about Price sunbathing in the nude.

'Many occasions'? Ah, so he does it a lot? So when the neighbour says that she 'saw something she did not expect' – not strictly true, is it?

But Mark McCone for Price of Scholes Park Road in Scarborough said Price had been mowing his lawn in a towel when he experienced problems with the mower. As he struggled with the machine, the towel fell off, leaving Price naked for a few moments before he changed into a pair of shorts and continued with the gardening.

■

Nice try, but I'm sorry, that simply won't hold up in court.

Lift Fall Man Hits Woman

Daily Record (April)

A man who plunged 25 ft down a lift shaft ...

... had his fall broken by a woman who had fallen down the day before.

Jens Wilhelms, 27, managed to free himself, but the 57-year-old woman he landed on was badly injured and is critical in hospital.
■

Lift Fall Man? Is he another of these obscure superheroes? 'Oh no, that lady's tripped over and is prostrate on the pavement! Don't panic – send for "Lift Fall Man", he'll use his special powers to lift her back up again!'

Oh, gotcha – should have read on.

You know what? Some people are born under a lucky star. You fall down a lift shaft and in those milliseconds of rapid descent, you must think, 'I'm a dead man,' and then ... bumf! You land on top of a woman.

By the way, where I come from a man falling on top of an unconscious woman is also called 'marriage'.

The question, of course, is: how stupid do you have to be to fall down a lift shaft? By definition, the shaft doors must have been open, right? Now I can understand that one idiot might think that because the doors were open, the lift was there and just happened to resemble a gaping chasm – but two people in two days?!

I think this is something more sinister. I think it was a trap. Someone left the doors open on purpose and when an understandably curious person or persons ventured to look down the lift shaft ... push! 'Ah ha, April fool!' (Bit late on the 16th, admittedly, but hey.)

Or theory number two: the bloke pushed her down, then lost his balance and fell in on top of her.

Or theory number three: it's a couple whose 'let's shaft in a lift shaft' fetish went horribly wrong.

NON-DRIVER CRASHED CAR WHILE OVER LIMIT

Buxton Advertiser

Liam David Thomas had decided at 4 a.m. to go and buy some cigarettes.

He took car keys from the kitchen and drove his brother's Renault Clio to Tesco. On the way back, he missed the turning. He hit a kerb and a tree causing some damage. Kirsten Collins, defending, said, 'He can't actually provide any explanation why he did what he did.'

■

How did that happen? He couldn't drive *and* he was drunk? And he crashed?

At 4 a.m.!

So what's this, then? He wanted some fags so he drove to Tesco. It's an explanation, isn't it?

Nuke vet blast-off

Sunday Mirror

The ashes of a former Navy diver who took part in British nuclear bomb tests were attached to a torpedo then blasted into the sea. The Navy suggested the idea when 71-year-old Derick Redfern's widow Ann asked them to carry out his wish for his ashes to be scattered at sea. Ann, of Cornwall, said, 'It was exactly what Derick wanted.'

■

It was 'exactly' what he wanted? What? He said, 'When I die, I want my ashes scattered at sea.' So his wife Ann says, 'How exactly? From the cliff top? Off the ferry? From the end of the pier?' 'No,' he says, 'in the usual way. I want them strapped to a torpedo and fired out to sea.' Oh right!

I wish I'd read this before my Uncle George died; it would have saved a massive argument. You see, because he'd been in the Navy, half of the family wanted him buried at sea, but the other half wanted him cremated – and how they argued. Very heated it was: 'Buried at sea!' 'Cremated!' 'Buried at sea!' 'Cremated!' In the end, we compromised and had him poached.

'DOG PATIENT' DENTIST IS JAILED

© bbc.co.uk/news

A dentist and his wife who stole more than £30,000 from the NHS by claiming money for treatment never given to patients have been jailed. Newton Johnson, 52 ...

... and his wife Judith, 51, also claimed for treatment for 'phantom' patients.

Justin Gau, prosecuting, told the court how Newton Johnson's sister's pet dog, called Varlo, was on the list as Varlo Johnson.

Never trust anyone called Newton.

Ghosts? No wonder they got caught.

We've established the dentist's a total idiot and it obviously runs in the family. His sister has called her dog Varlo, which is a totally mad name for a dog. It sounds like an illusionist (as in 'The Amazing VARLO') or a toilet cleaner (as in, er ... 'The Amazing VARLO', probably).

201

Mr Gau added, 'They were saying to the public purse, "open wide," and performing a series of illegal extractions.

See what he did there? He's a card, isn't he, that young Mr Gau? Can't you just see him delivering that 'comic' line to the courtroom in a smug, self-congratulatory, barrister-like manner? I bet he's a riot at the parties in his chambers – not in court, clearly, where I bet the jurors and judge thought, 'Prick.'

'The fillings they performed were the fillings of their own wallets.'

Oh stop it, Mr Gau ... NO, I MEAN IT – STOP IT NOW. You've watched too much *Crown Court* and not enough *Judge John Deed*.

Mr Gau said that Johnson was unhappy in his work at the Inkerman Street practice in Llanelli and kept a diary.

I rest my case – complete and total idiot dentist. Ripped off the NHS and kept a diary about his feelings at the same time.

Some of the entries were read out in court.

This is great. Listen to this ...

He wrote, 'This bloody job — who would be a pigging dentist?'

I would. I'll have a go. Go on, let me. The money's brilliant, right? And how hard can it be? No, really, it's teeth. 'Which one hurts? This one?' 'Nargh.' 'This one?' 'Arrgghhhhh.' 'That'll have to come out.'

And then there's the power. You've got such power, such control. No one likes going to the dentist; most people are terrified. Think of the power when you pick up the drill and give it a zzzzzzzzzeeeeeeeeeee!

And you could have a right laugh at the expense of your more obnoxious patients. Tell them they need an extraction, then tie a piece of string to the tooth and open the door and tie the other end to the doorknob. See how far you can get before they freak out. You never know, just occasionally you might even get to slam the door – see if it actually works!

Or what about getting them under the anaesthetic ... and then blacking out their front teeth with a felt tip?

Another entry, 'You have to laugh. Burned a patient's lip this morning.'

You do. You have to laugh, it's funny; far funnier than Mr Gau and his crap double entendres. Burning somebody's lip is brilliant. Be great if he was using matches to look in the patient's mouth, wouldn't it? 'Very dark in here' ... ouch.

Another entry, 'I hate my work so much. I drink it away. I loathe it.'

Is he drinking that pink mouthwash? I mean, that would explain a lot.

After the NHS began its probe, another entry read, 'We are in deep shit now.'
■

What? Where are they probing?! Wrong end by the sound of it.

Briton arrested for sex attacks on sheep

© Reuters

A Briton has been arrested on suspicion of carrying out a series of sex attacks on sheep, London police said on Friday. The 27-year-old man was held at his home in Dulwich, south London on suspicion of bestiality with sheep.

Sheep in Dulwich? Surely not. Are they sure it wasn't a fat lass in an Aran sweater?

He was also wanted in connection with the possession of drugs with intent to supply.

See, kids, this is a powerful reason to 'just say no': drugs make sheep look gorgeous.

Two male joggers said they had observed a man molesting the sheep in a field in Botany Bay Lane, Chislehurst. Media reports said the man had been barred from visiting farmland.

'Barred'?! Well done.

MAN ACCUSED OF SEX WITH FELTHAM HORSE GETS OFF WITH CAUTION

www.thisislocallondon.co.uk

A man in his sixties who was arrested after allegedly having sex with a horse in a Feltham field is set to escape with a caution, Hounslow police said this week. The suspect was questioned by officers on Friday 8 August after drivers claimed they saw him performing an indecent act on the animal near the A30.

That's how I'd get off a horse – with caution. They can be very unpredictable.

A night of 'unbridled' passion in a field next to a busy 'A' road ... how mad is that? Well, I mean if having sex with a horse isn't mad enough.

Detective Inspector Jeff Minns said police had no intention of charging the man and were due to caution him for cruelty to animals.

■

Cruelty? Prove it.

And I'm proud to say that I never used the word 'Feltham'. Well, until now.

ACKNOWLEDGEMENTS

The author and publishers would especially like to thank the news agencies and newspapers who have permitted the use of their articles in this book, including:

The Bolton News; *Buxton Advertiser*; *Daily Mirror*/Mirrorpix; *Daily Record*; *Daily Telegraph*; *Denbighshire Visitor*; *Derbyshire Times*; *Derry Journal*; *Evening Chronicle, Newcastle*; *Evening Times, Glasgow*; *Halifax Evening Courier*; *Herts Advertiser*; *Hull Daily Mail*; *The Hutchinson News*; *Irish Independent*; *Lancashire Evening Post*; *Lancaster Guardian*; *Leamington Spa Courier*; *Leicester Mercury*; *Liverpool Daily Post*; *Liverpool Echo*; *News & Star, Carlisle*; *North Wales Daily Post*; *Northants Evening Telegraph*; *The Northern Echo*; *Oldham Advertiser*; *Oldham Evening Chronicle*; *Outlook* Magazine; *The Press, York*; *Skegness Standard*; *Skegness Target*; *Stockport Express*; *The Sun*/NI Syndication; *Sunday Mirror*/Mirrorpix; *Sunderland Echo*; *The Times*/NI Syndication; *Warrington Guardian*; *Weston & Somerset Mercury*; *Wrexham Leader*; www.thisislocallondon.co.uk; *Yorkshire Evening Post*.

Pages 11–13, 39–40, 53–4 and 153–4: News articles © Telegraph Media Group Limited.

Pages 73–5: News article reprinted with the express permission of: "CANWEST NEWS SERVICE", a CanWest Partnership.

Page 205: News article © Copyright 2008 Reuters. Reprinted with permission from Reuters. Reuters content is the intellectual property of Reuters or its third party content providers. Any copying, republication or redistribution of Reuters content is expressly prohibited without the prior written consent of Reuters. Reuters shall not be liable for any errors or delays in content, or for any actions taken in reliance thereon. Reuters and the Reuters Sphere Logo are registered trademarks of the Reuters group of companies around the world. For additional information about Reuters content and services, please visit Reuters website at www.reuters.com. License # REU-5749-MES.